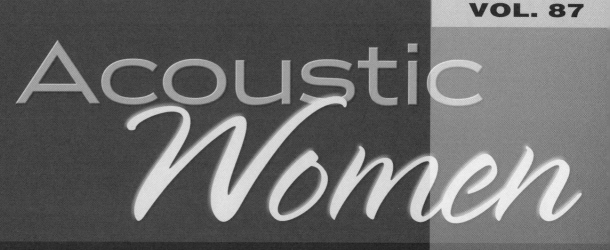

VOL. 87

HAL•LEONARD

GUITAR PLAY-ALONG

Acoustic Women

ISBN 978-1-4234-4318-6

HAL•LEONARD®
CORPORATION
7777 W. BLUEMOUND RD. P.O. BOX 13819 MILWAUKEE, WI 53213

Visit Hal Leonard Online at
www.halleonard.com

Acoustic Women

CONTENTS

Guitar Notation Legend

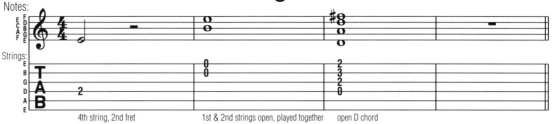

THE MUSICAL STAFF shows pitches and rhythms and is divided by bar lines into measures. Pitches are named after the first seven letters of the alphabet.

TABLATURE graphically represents the guitar fingerboard. Each horizontal line represents a string, and each number represents a fret.

4th string, 2nd fret   1st & 2nd strings open, played together   open D chord

HALF-STEP BEND: Strike the note and bend up 1/2 step.

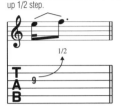

WHOLE-STEP BEND: Strike the note and bend up one step.

GRACE NOTE BEND: Strike the note and bend up as indicated. The first note does not take up any time.

SLIGHT (MICROTONE) BEND: Strike the note and bend up 1/4 step.

BEND AND RELEASE: Strike the note and bend up as indicated, then release back to the original note. Only the first note is struck.

PRE-BEND: Bend the note as indicated, then strike it.

VIBRATO: The string is vibrated by rapidly bending and releasing the note with the fretting hand.

PALM MUTING: The note is partially muted by the pick hand lightly touching the string(s) just before the bridge.

HAMMER-ON: Strike the first (lower) note with one finger, then sound the higher note (on the same string) with another finger by fretting it without picking.

PULL-OFF: Place both fingers on the notes to be sounded. Strike the first note and without picking, pull the finger off to sound the second (lower) note.

LEGATO SLIDE: Strike the first note and then slide the same fret-hand finger up or down to the second note. The second note is not struck.

SHIFT SLIDE: Same as legato slide, except the second note is struck.

TRILL: Very rapidly alternate between the notes indicated by continuously hammering on and pulling off.

TAPPING: Hammer ("tap") the fret indicated with the pick-hand index or middle finger and pull off to the note fretted by the fret hand.

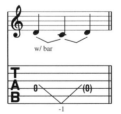

NATURAL HARMONIC: Strike the note while the fret-hand lightly touches the string directly over the fret indicated.

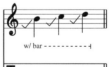

PINCH HARMONIC: The note is fretted normally and a harmonic is produced by adding the edge of the thumb or the tip of the index finger of the pick hand to the normal pick attack.

TREMOLO PICKING: The note is picked as rapidly and continuously as possible.

VIBRATO BAR DIVE AND RETURN: The pitch of the note or chord is dropped a specified number of steps (in rhythm) then returned to the original pitch.

VIBRATO BAR SCOOP: Depress the bar just before striking the note, then quickly release the bar.

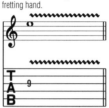

VIBRATO BAR DIP: Strike the note and then immediately drop a specified number of steps, then release back to the original pitch.

Additional Musical Definitions

 (accent) • Accentuate note (play it louder)

(staccato) • Play the note short

D.S. al Coda • Go back to the sign (%), then play until the measure marked "***To Coda***," then skip to the section labelled "***Coda***."

D.C. al Fine • Go back to the beginning of the song and play until the measure marked "***Fine***" (end).

Fill • Label used to identify a brief melodic figure which is to be inserted into the arrangement.

N.C. • No Chord

 • Repeat measures between signs.

  • When a repeated section has different endings, play the first ending only the first time and the second ending only the second time.

5

Adia

Words and Music by Sarah McLachlan and Pierre Marchand

Capo III

Verse
Moderately slow ♩ = 78

*Symbols in parentheses represent chord names respective to capoed guitar.
Symbols above represent actual sounding chords. Capoed fret is "0" in tab.

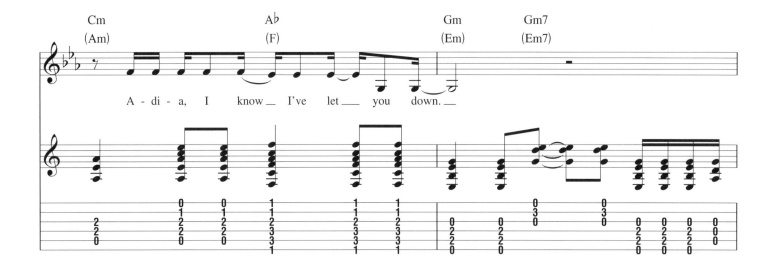

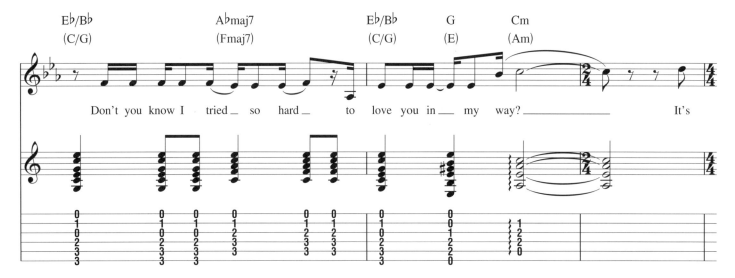

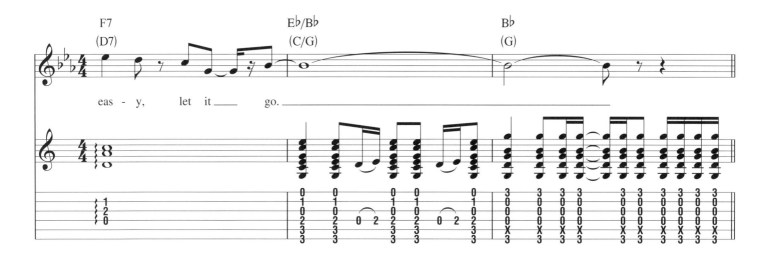

eas - y, let it ___ go. ___

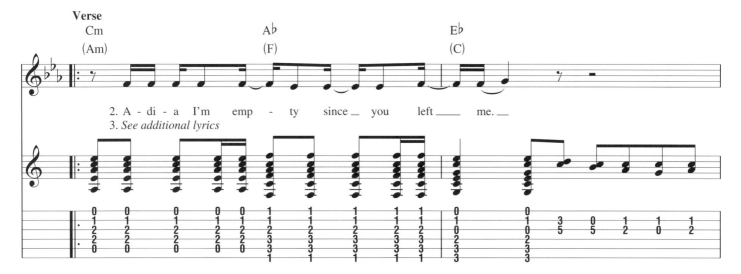

Verse

2. A - di - a I'm emp - ty since ___ you left ___ me. ___
3. *See additional lyrics*

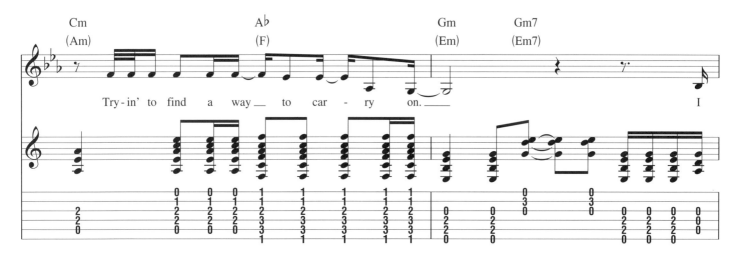

Try - in' to find a way ___ to car - ry on. ___ I

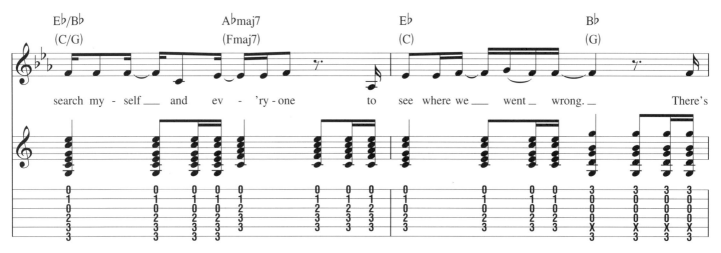

search my - self ___ and ev - 'ry - one to see where we ___ went ___ wrong. ___ There's

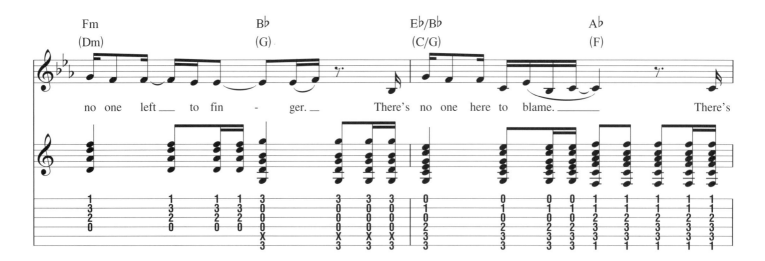

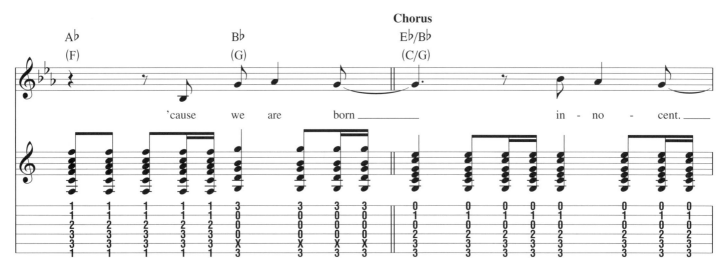

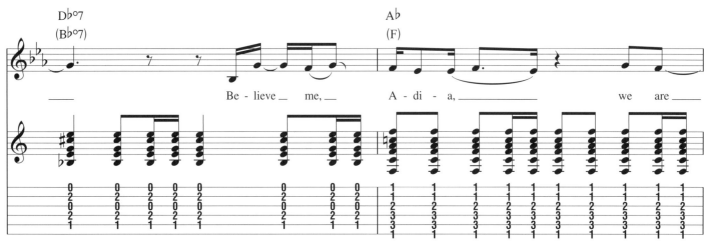

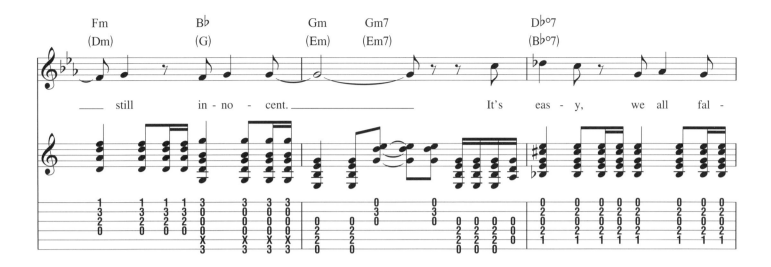

still in-no-cent. _____ It's eas-y, we all fal-

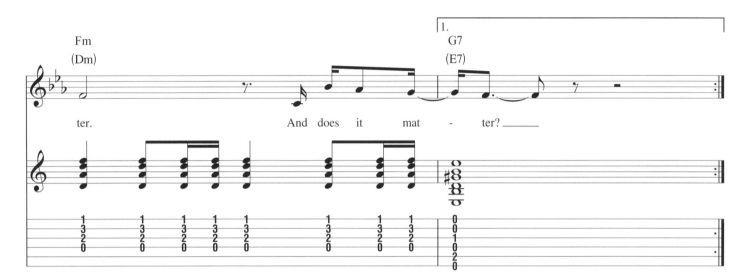

1.

ter. And does it mat-ter? _____

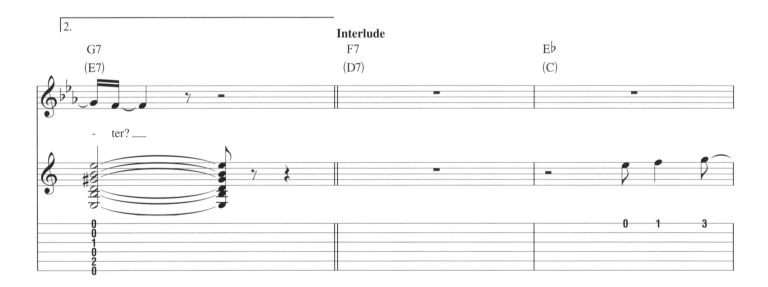

2.

Interlude

- ter? ___

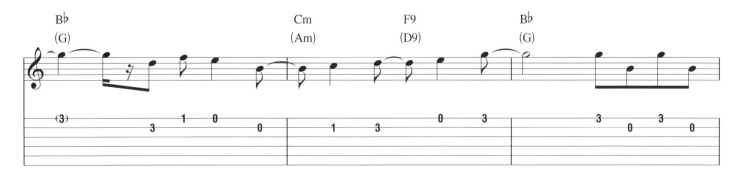

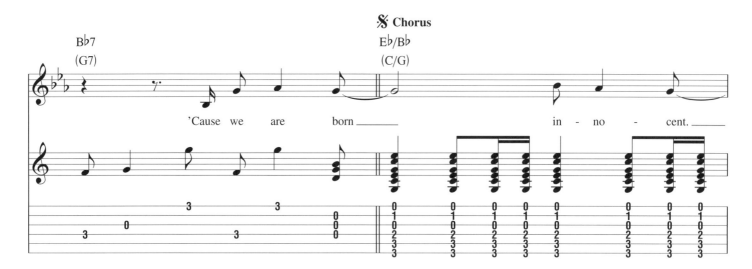

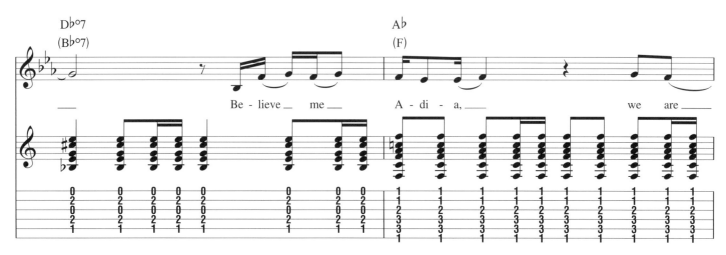

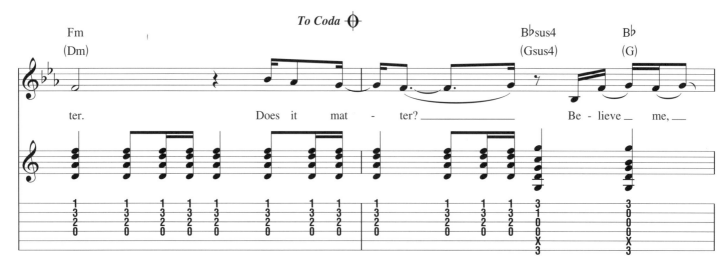

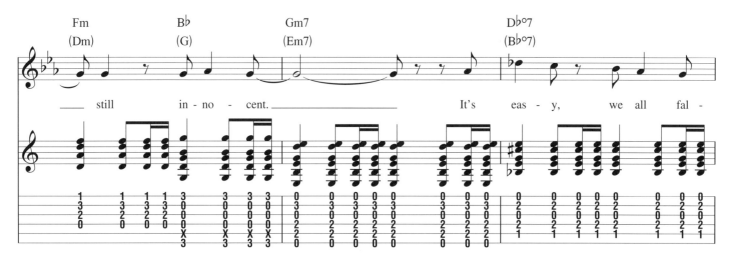

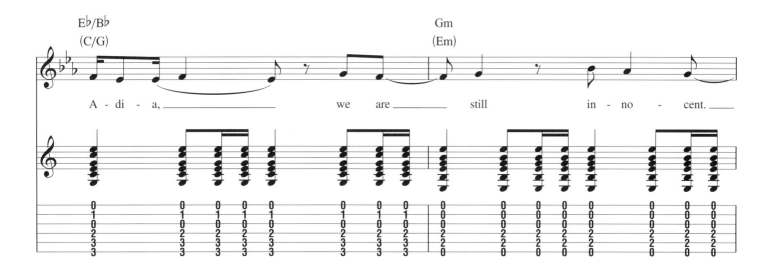

D.S. al Coda

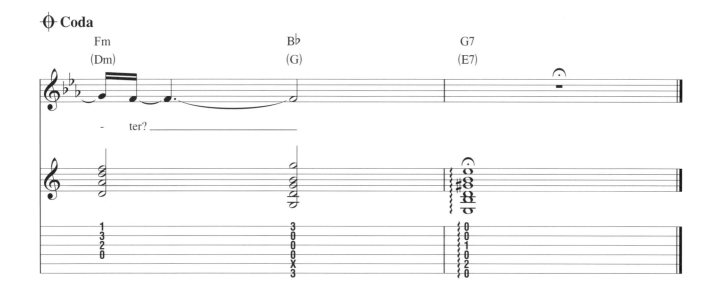

Additional Lyrics

3. Adia I thought that we could make it.
I know I can't change the way you feel.
I leave you with your misery, a friend who won't betray.
Pull you from your tower. I take away your pain.
I show you all the beauty you possess,
If you'd only let yourself believe that we are born...

Closer to Fine

Words and Music by Emily Saliers

Capo II

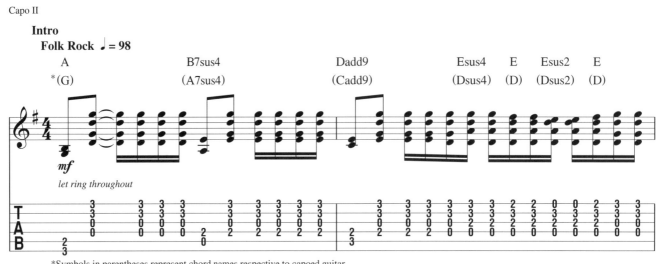

*Symbols in parentheses represent chord names respective to capoed guitar.
Symbols above reflect actual sounding chords. Capoed fret is "0" in tab.

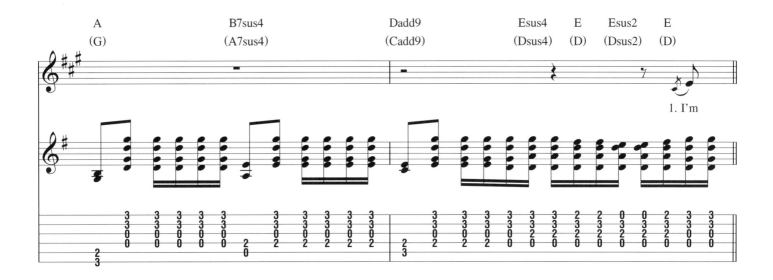

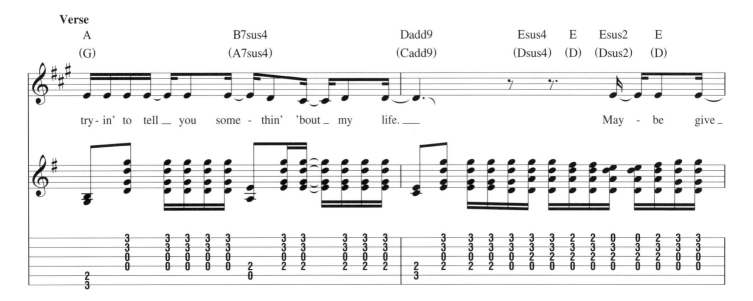

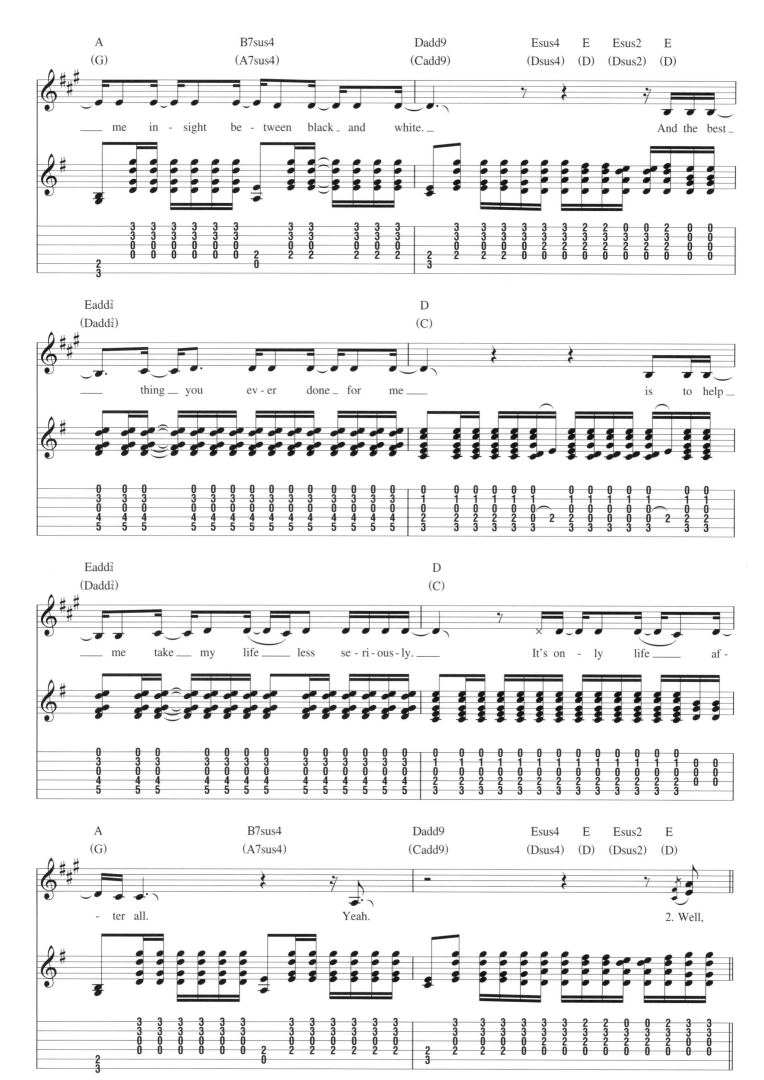

Verse

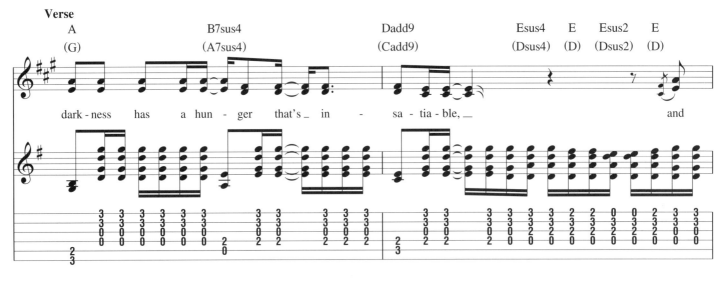

darkness has a hun-ger that's _ in - sa - tia - ble, _ and

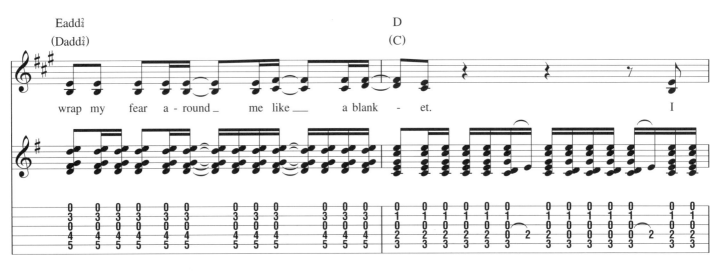

light-ness has a call _ that's hard to hear. _ And I'll

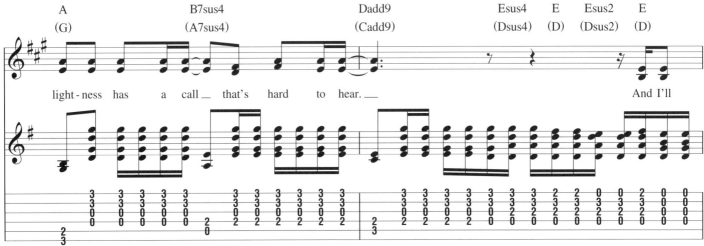

wrap my fear a-round _ me like _ a blank - et. I

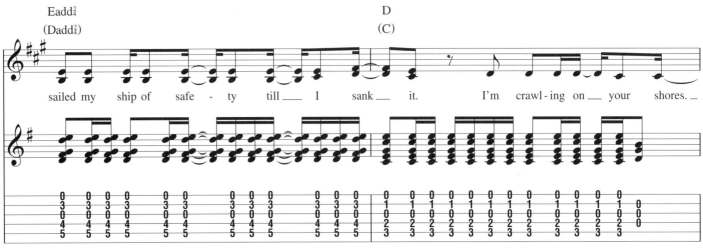

sailed my ship of safe-ty till _ I sank _ it. I'm crawl-ing on _ your shores. _

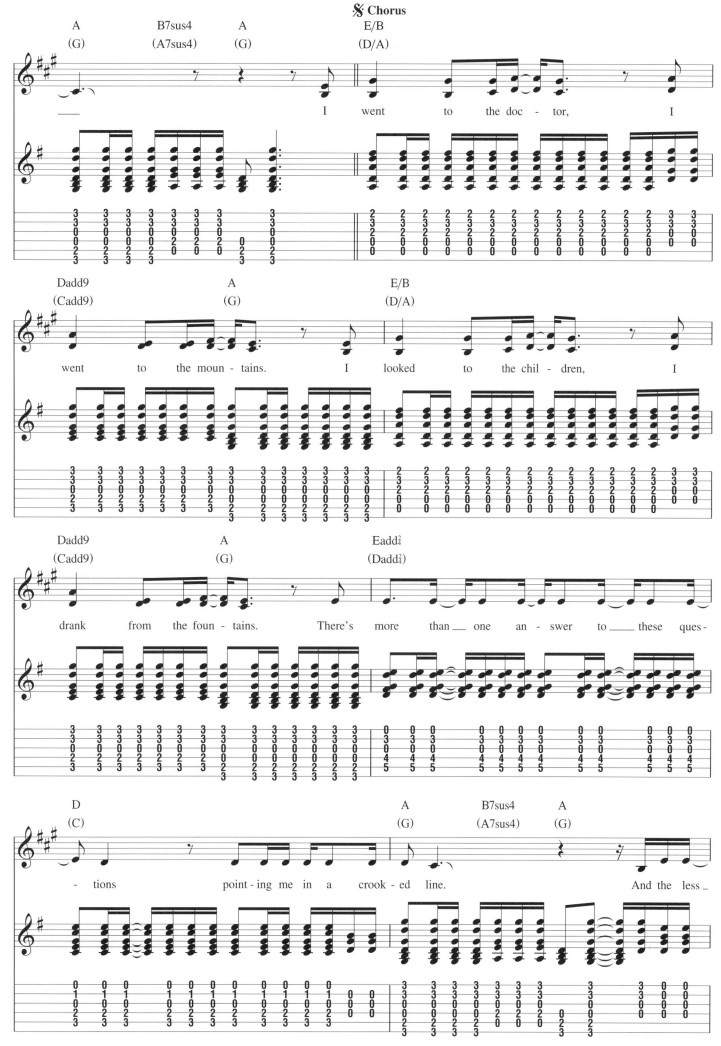

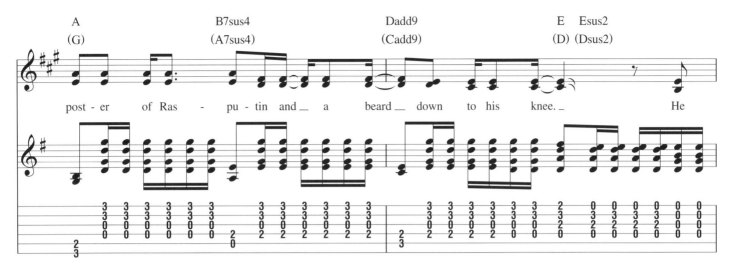

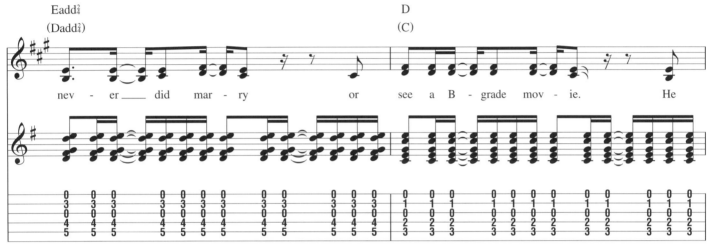

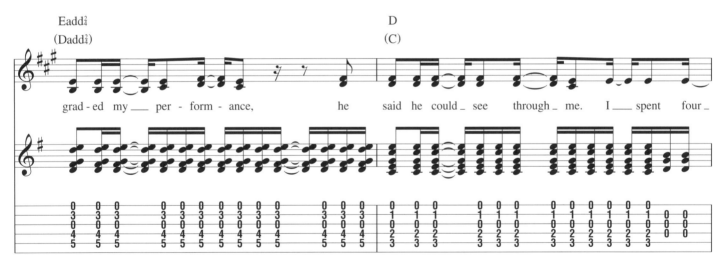

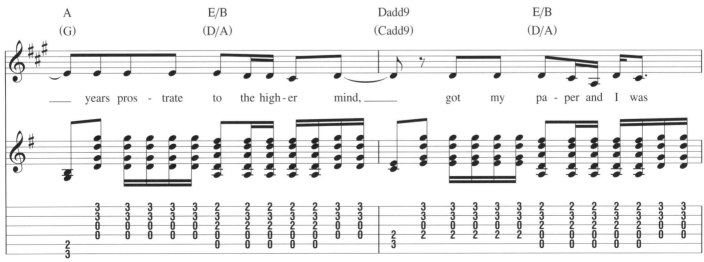

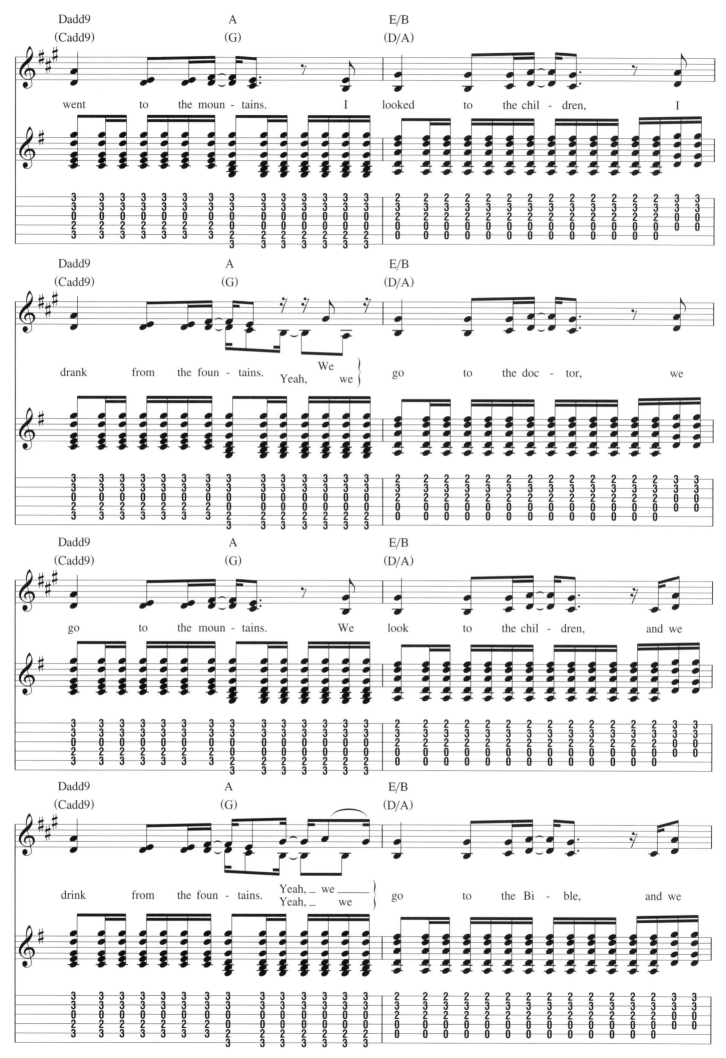

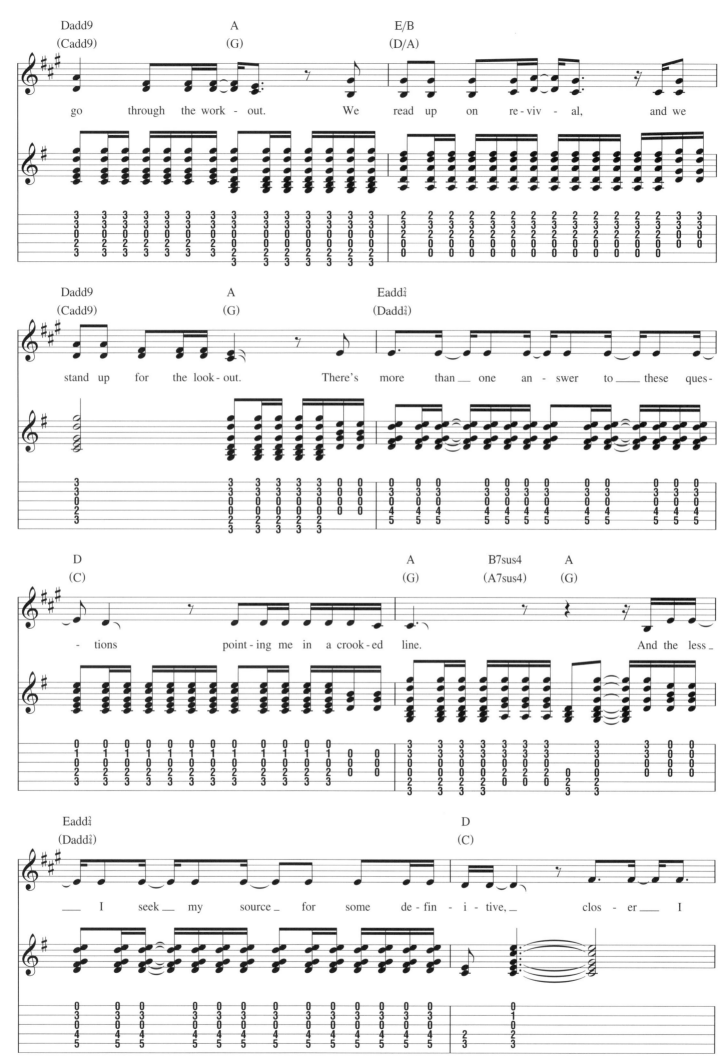

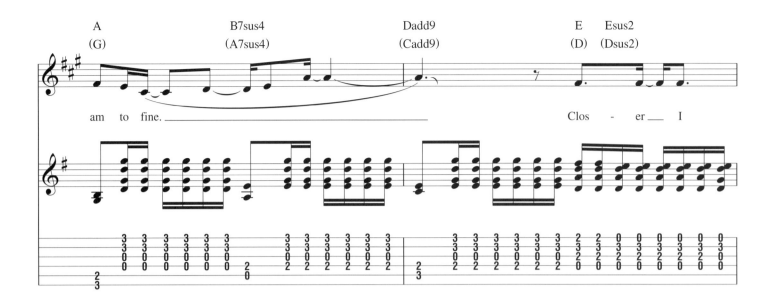

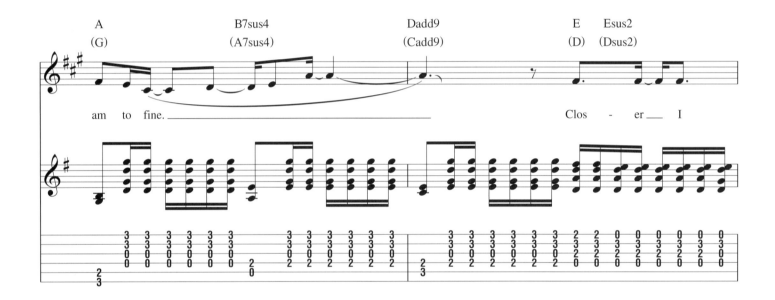

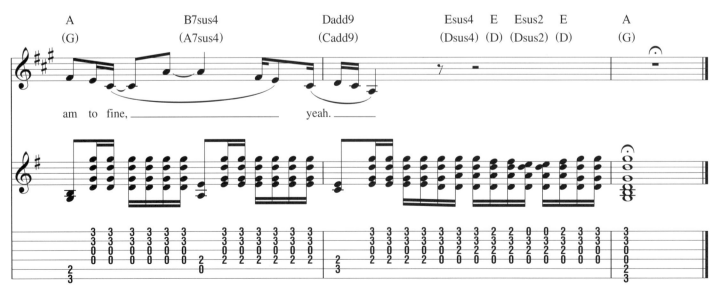

Dadd9
(Cadd9)
A
(G)
E/B
(D/A)
go through the work - out. We read up on re - viv - al, and we
Dadd9
(Cadd9)
A
(G)
Eadd2/4
(Dadd2/4)
stand up for the look - out. There's more than one an - swer to these ques-
D
(C)
A
(G)
B7sus4
(A7sus4)
A
(G)
- tions point - ing me in a crook - ed line. And the less
Eadd2/4
(Dadd2/4)
D
(C)
I seek my source for some de - fin - i - tive, clos - er I

If It Makes You Happy

Words and Music by Jeff Trott and Sheryl Crow

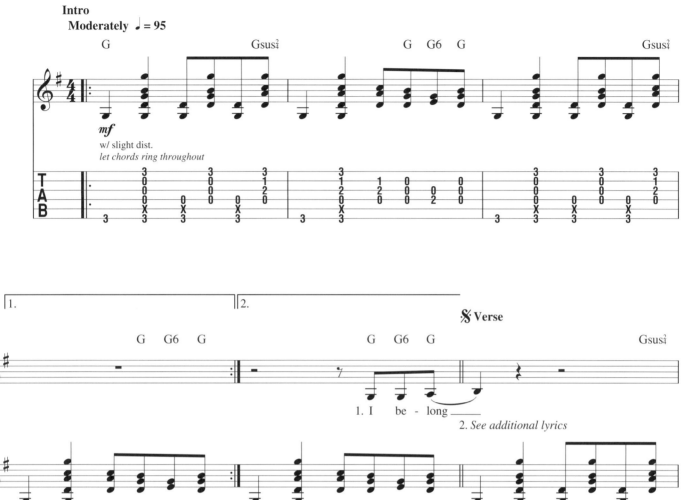

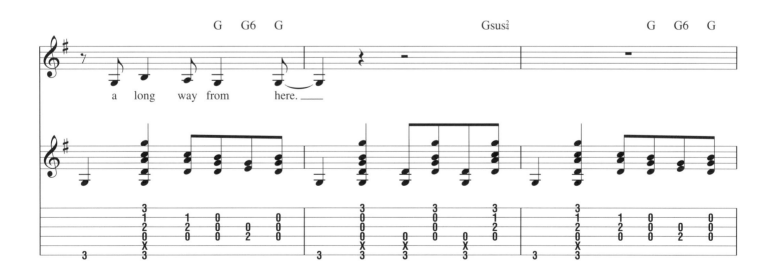

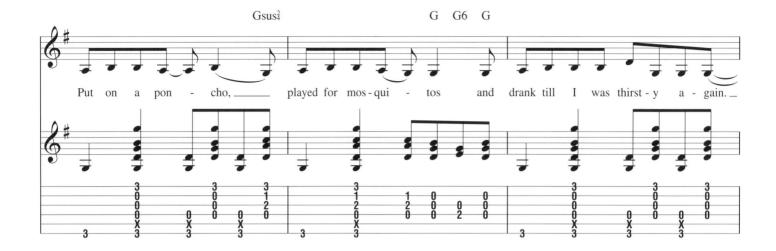

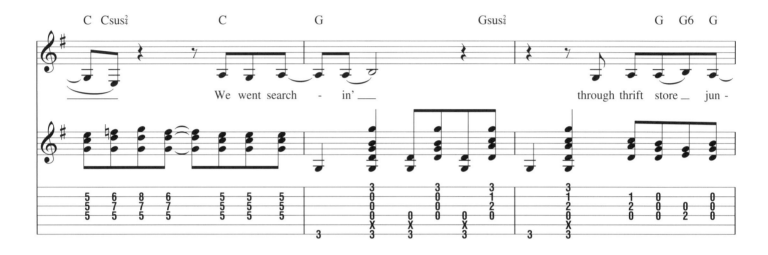

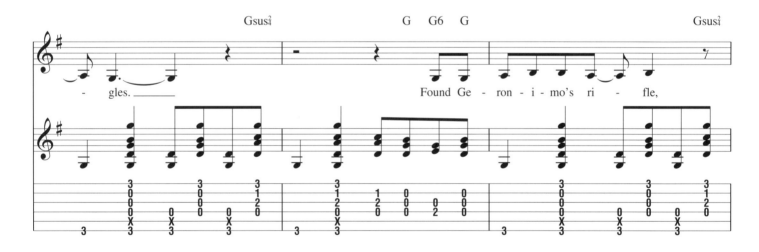

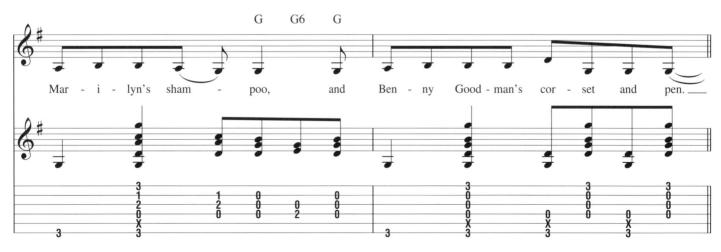

Pre-Chorus

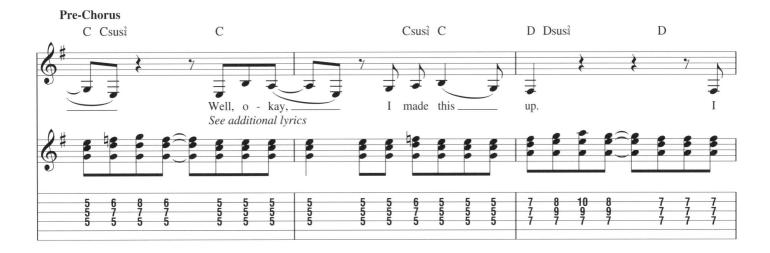

Well, o - kay, _____ I made this _____ up.
See additional lyrics

I

To Coda 1

Chorus

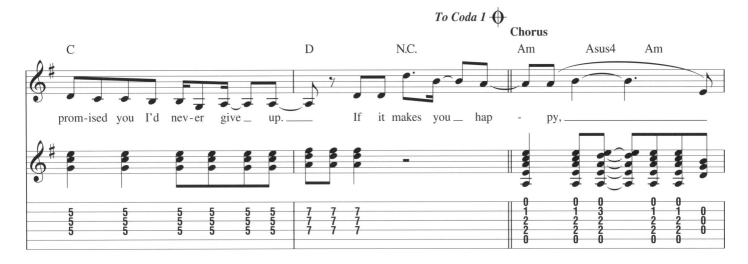

prom-ised you I'd nev-er give _ up. _____ If it makes you _ hap - py, _____

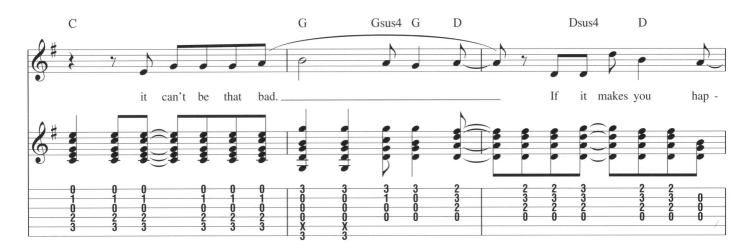

it can't be that bad. _____ If it makes you hap -

Interlude

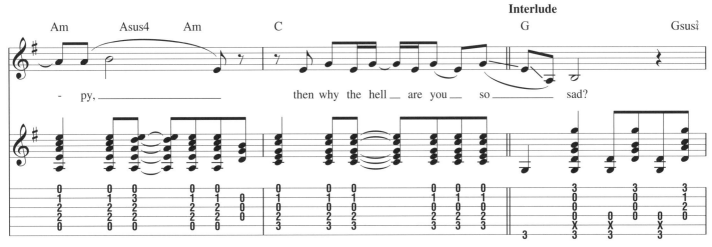

- py, _____ then why the hell _ are you _ so _____ sad?

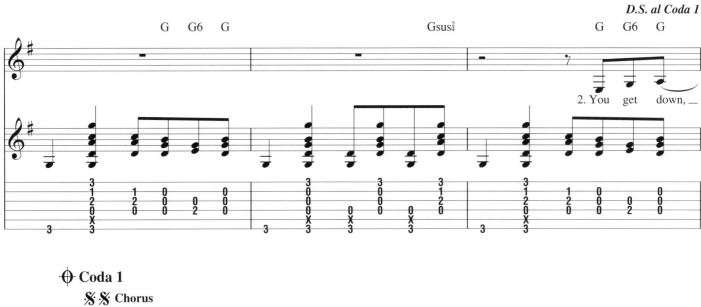

Coda 1

Chorus

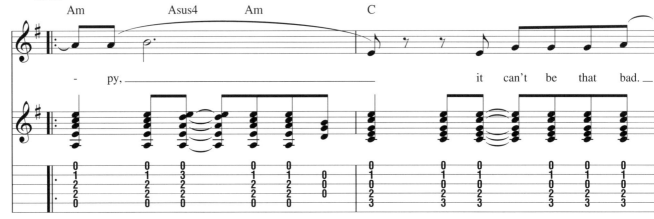

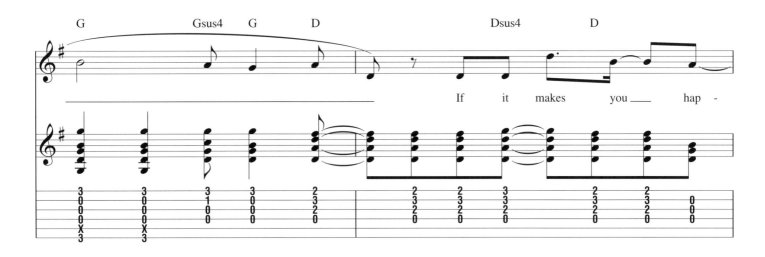

4th time, To Coda 2

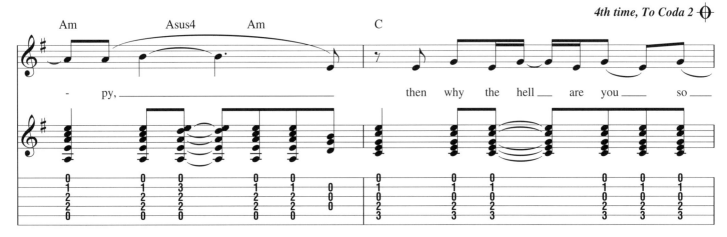

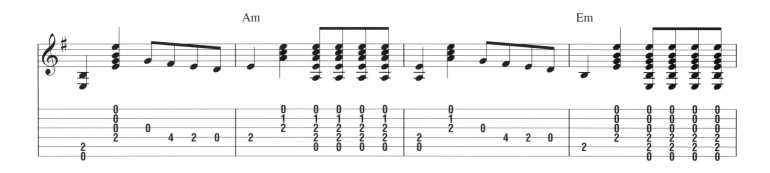

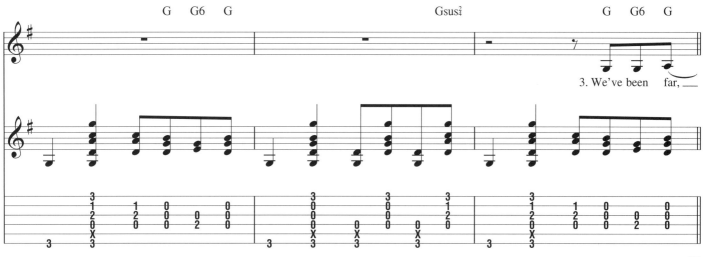

Verse

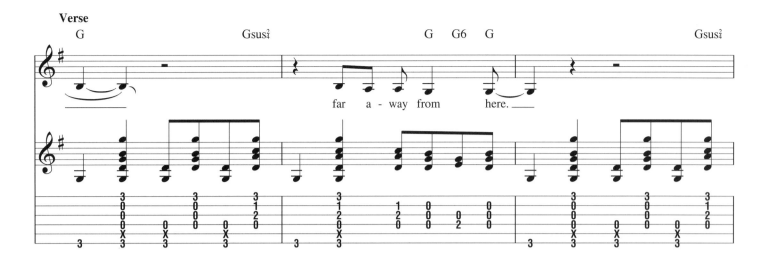

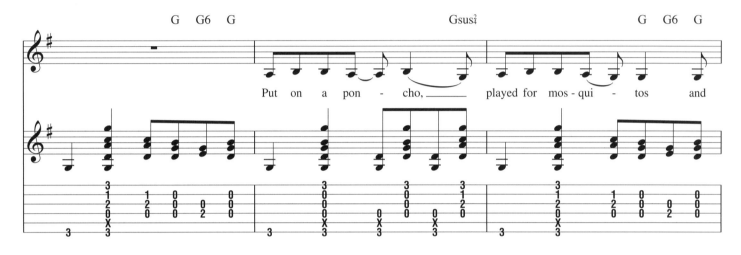

Pre-Chorus

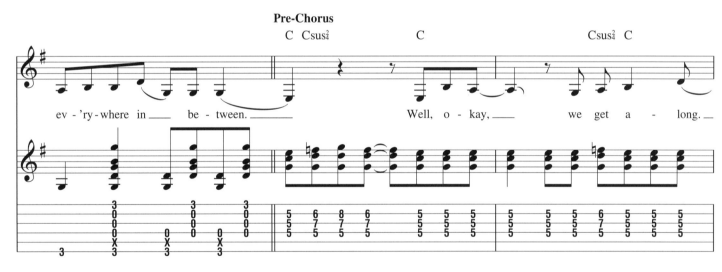

Coda 2

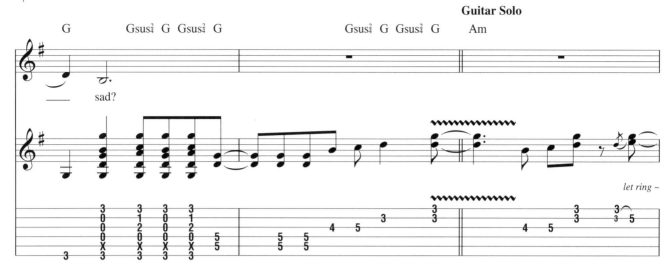

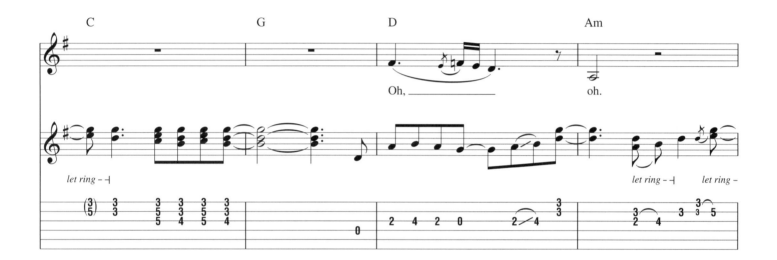

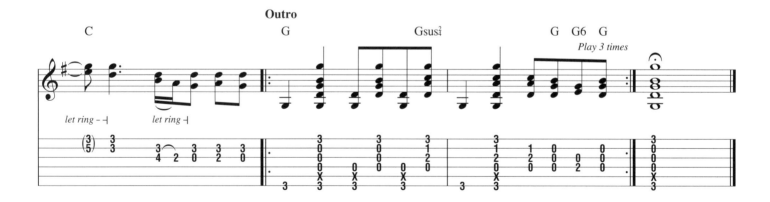

Additional Lyrics

2. You get down, a, real low down.
   You listen to Coltrane, derail your own train.
   Well, who hasn't been there before?
   I come 'round, around the hard way.
   Bring comics in bed, scrape the mold off the bread
   And serve you french toast again.

Pre-Chorus Well, okay, I still get stoned.
   I'm not the kind of girl you take home.

Ironic

Lyrics by Alanis Morissette
Music by Alanis Morissette and Glen Ballard

Capo IV

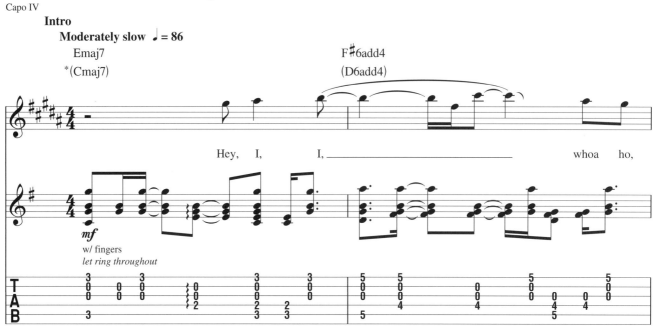

*Symbols in parentheses represent chord names respective to capoed guitar.
Symbols above reflect actual sounding chords. Capoed fret is "0" in tab.

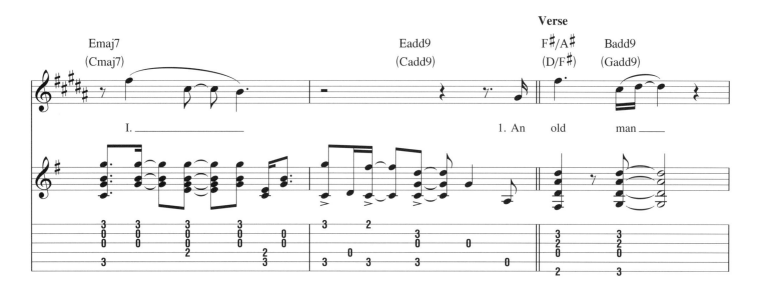

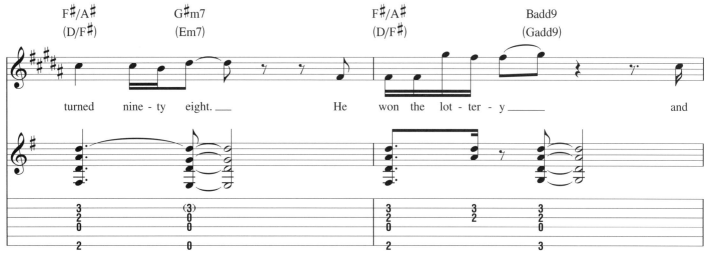

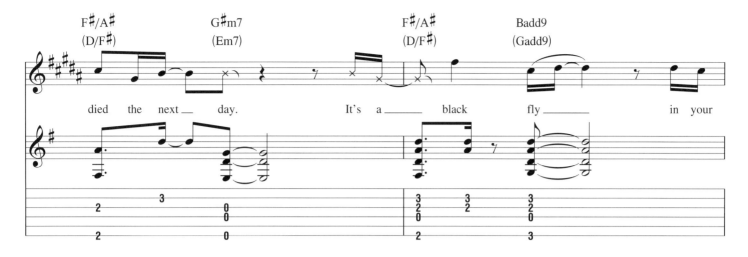

died the next ___ day.   It's a ___ black   fly ___ in your

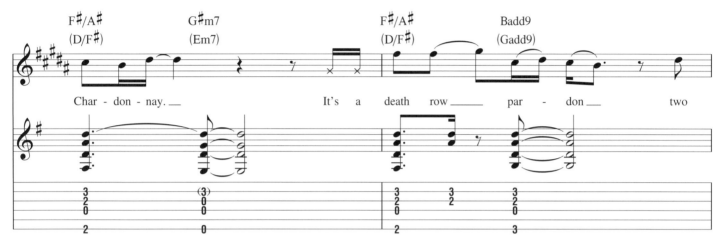

Char - don - nay. ___   It's a death row ___ par - don ___ two

Pre-Chorus

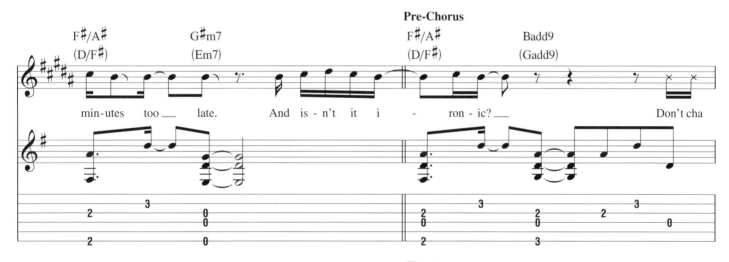

min - utes too ___ late.   And is - n't it i - ron - ic? ___   Don't cha

Chorus

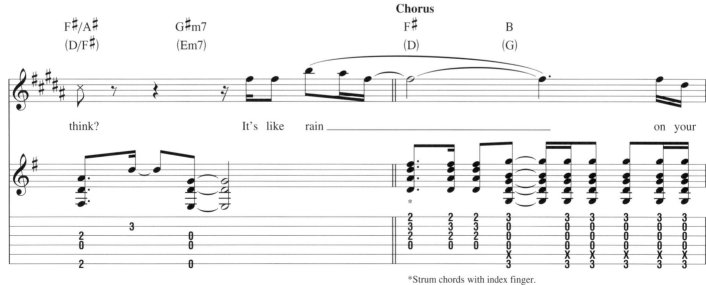

think?   It's like   rain _____ on your

*Strum chords with index finger.

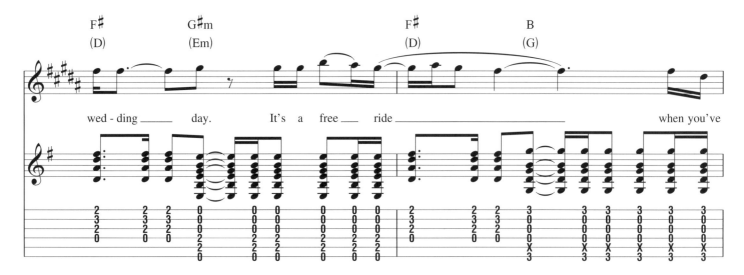

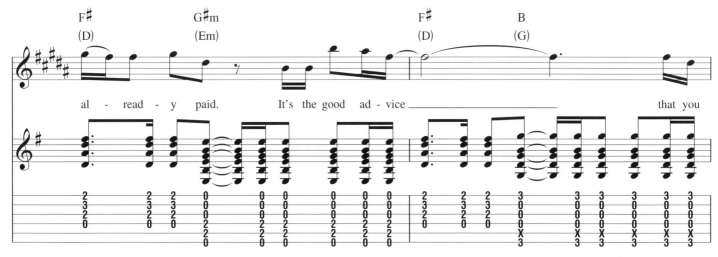

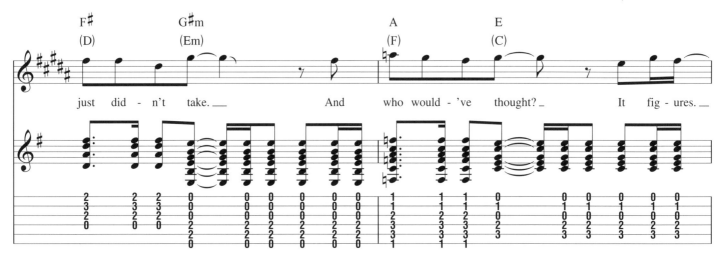

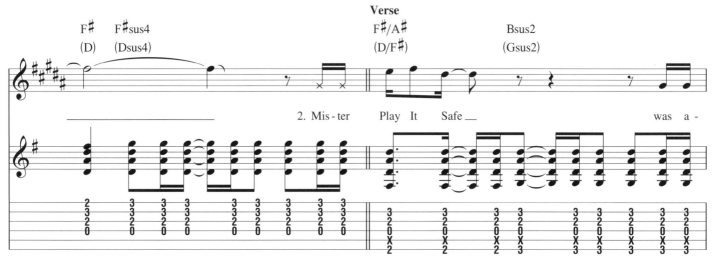

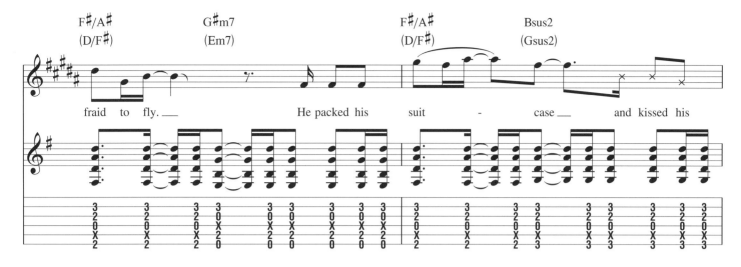

fraid to fly. ___ He packed his suit - case ___ and kissed his

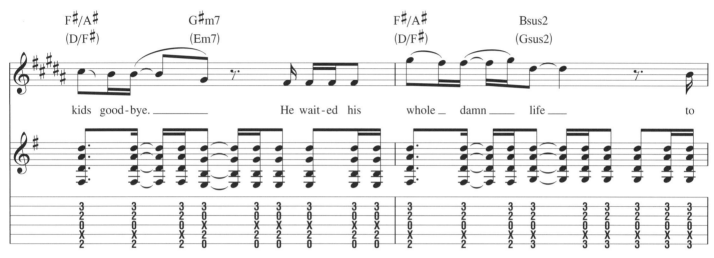

kids good-bye. _____ He wait-ed his whole _ damn ___ life ___ to

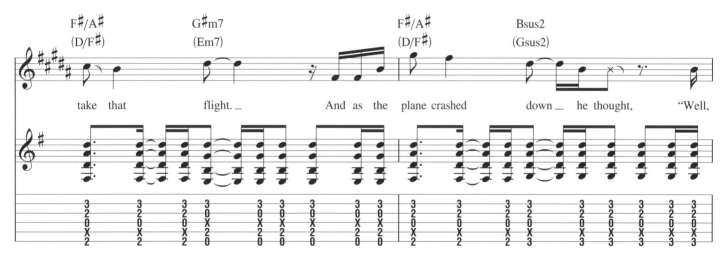

take that flight. _ And as the plane crashed down _ he thought, "Well,

Pre-Chorus

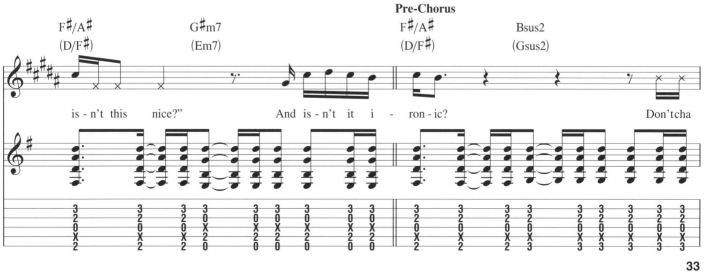

is - n't this nice?" And is - n't it i - ron - ic? Don'tcha

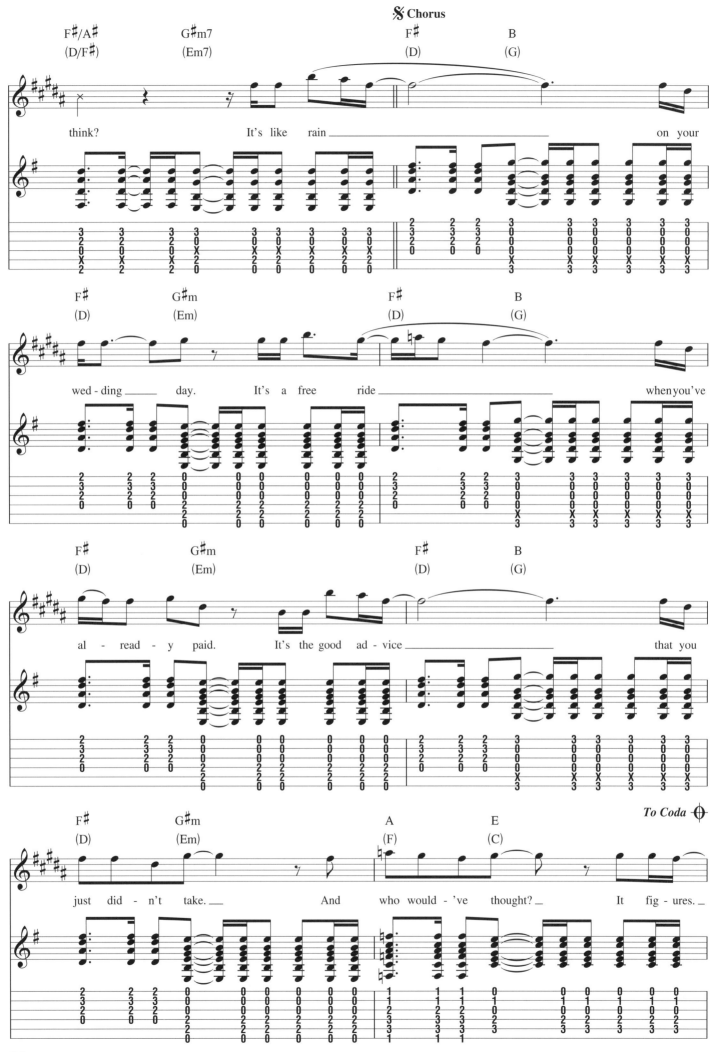

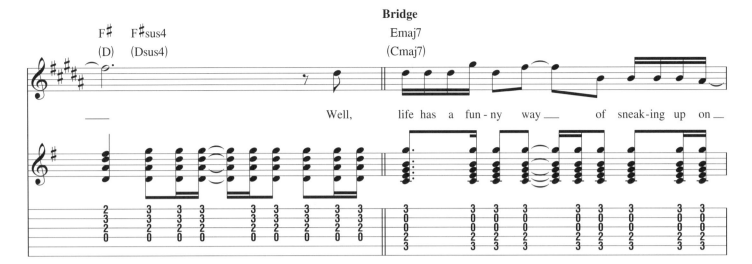

Well, life has a fun-ny way __ of sneak-ing up on __

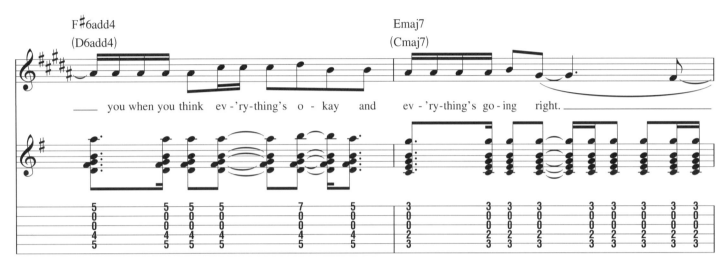

__ you when you think ev-'ry-thing's o - kay and ev-'ry-thing's go-ing right. _____

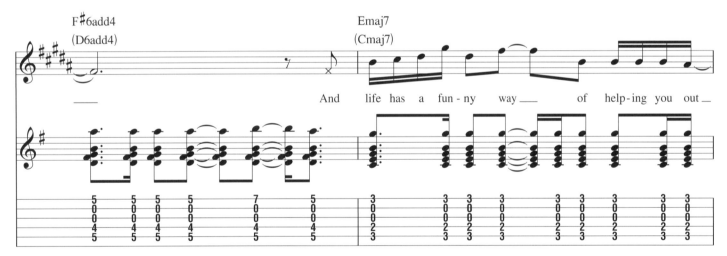

__ And life has a fun-ny way __ of help-ing you out __

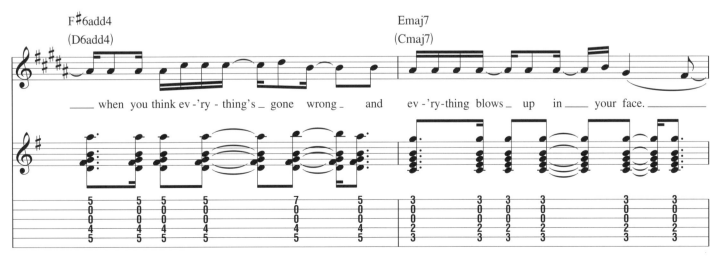

__ when you think ev-'ry - thing's __ gone wrong __ and ev-'ry-thing blows __ up in __ your face. ___

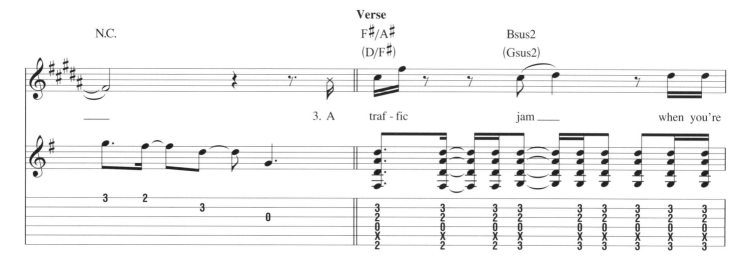

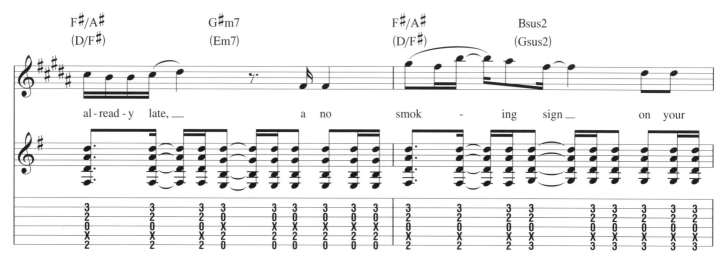

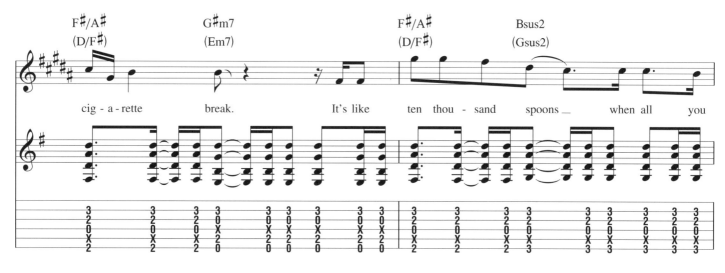

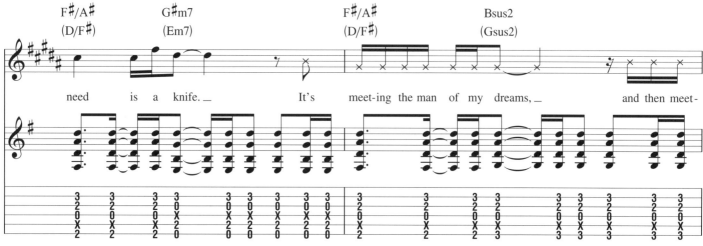

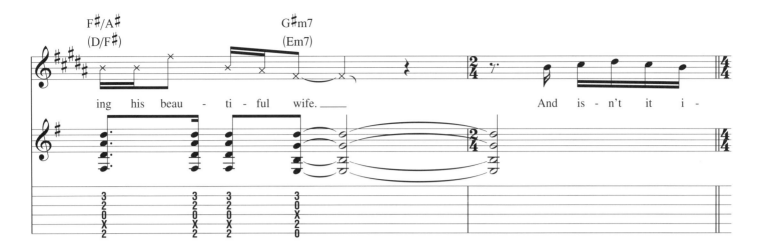

Pre-Chorus

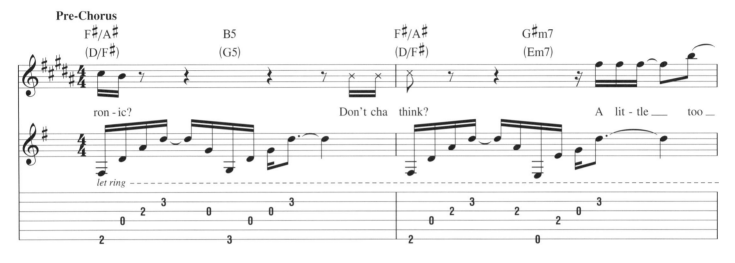

D.S. al Coda

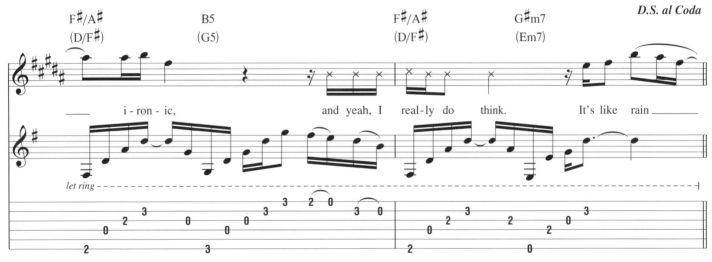

Coda

Bridge

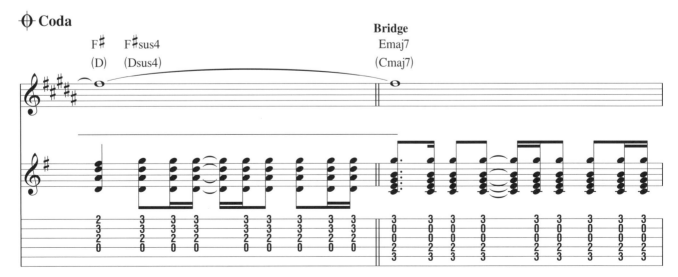

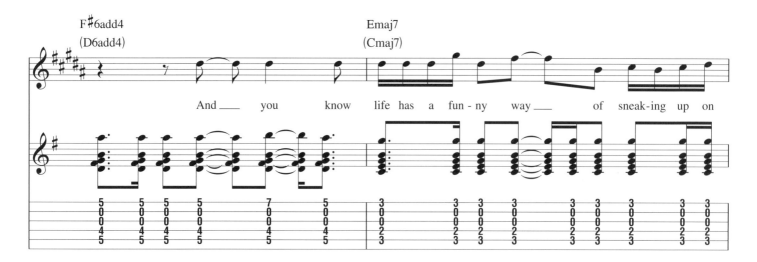

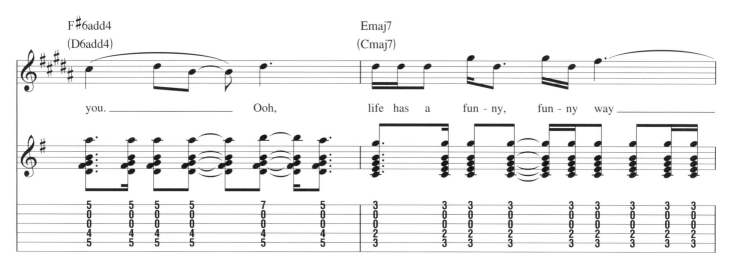

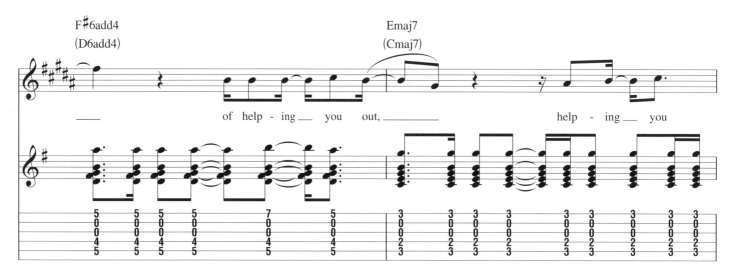

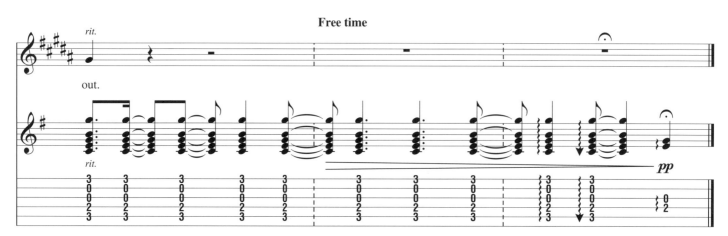

Like the Way I Do

Words and Music by Melissa Etheridge

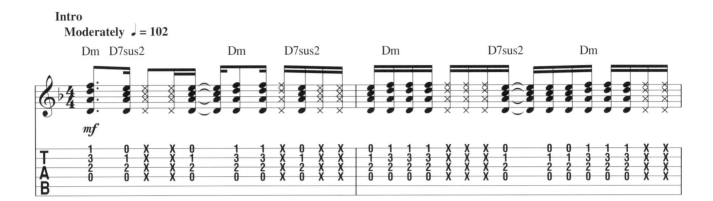

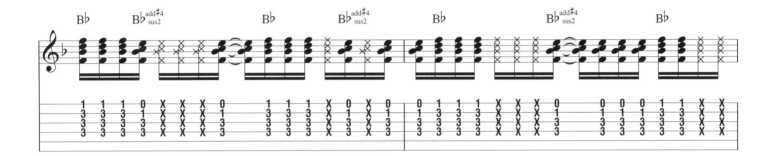

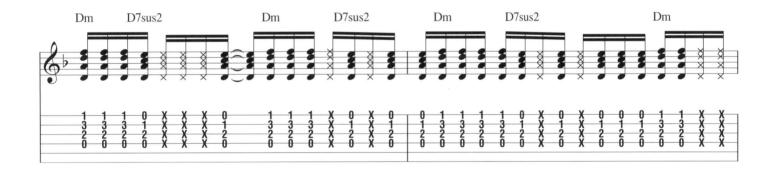

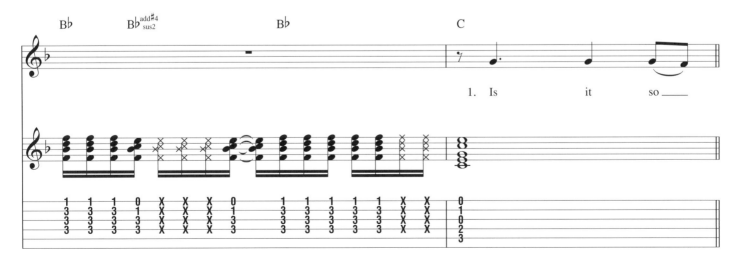

Verse

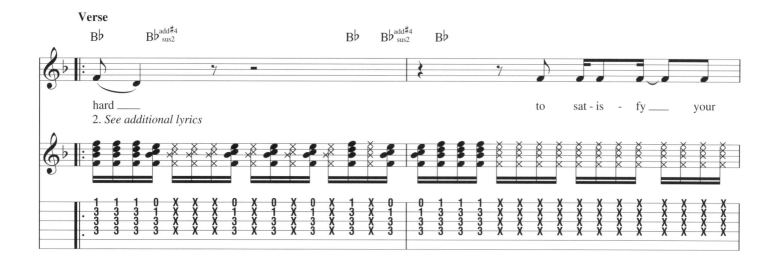

hard ___

2. See additional lyrics

to sat - is - fy ___ your

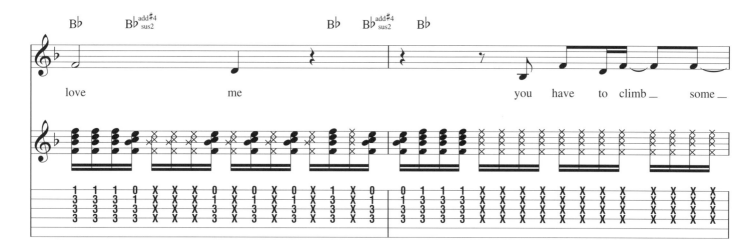

sens - es. ___

You found out to

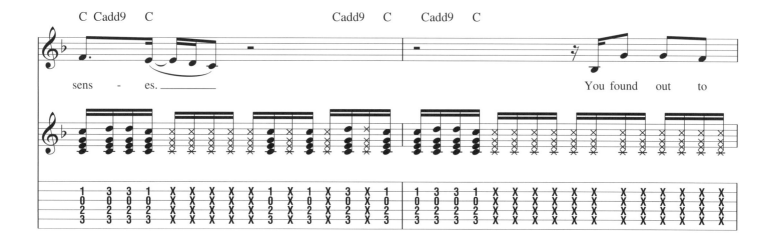

love me you have to climb ___ some ___

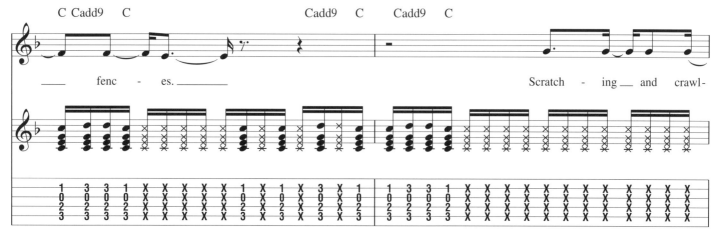

___ fenc - es. ___

Scratch - ing ___ and crawl-

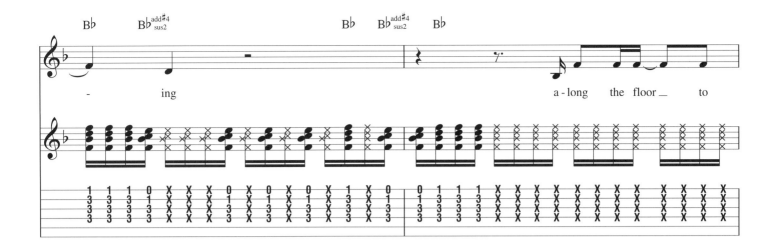

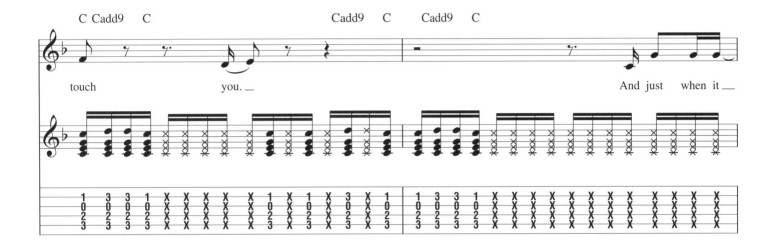

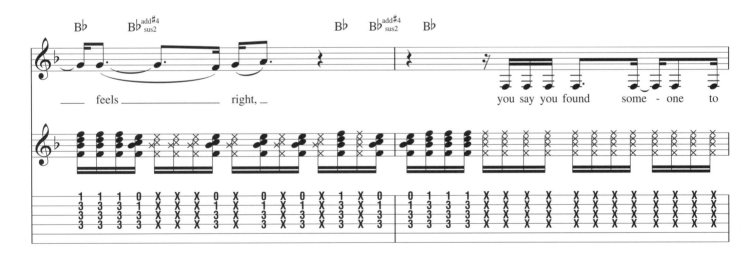

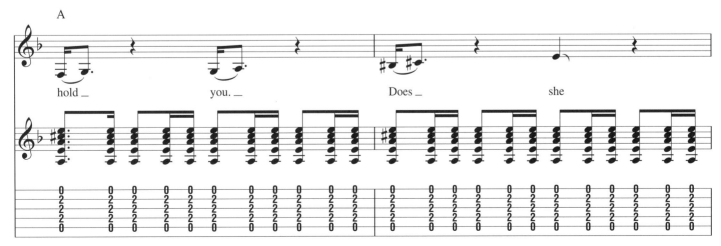

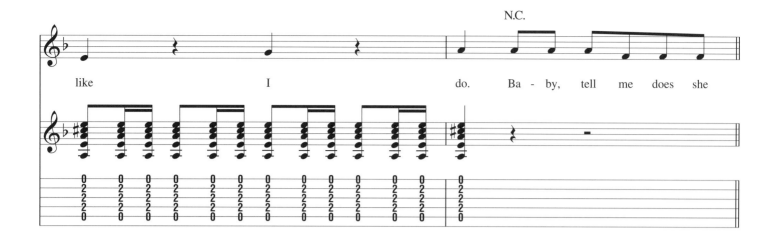

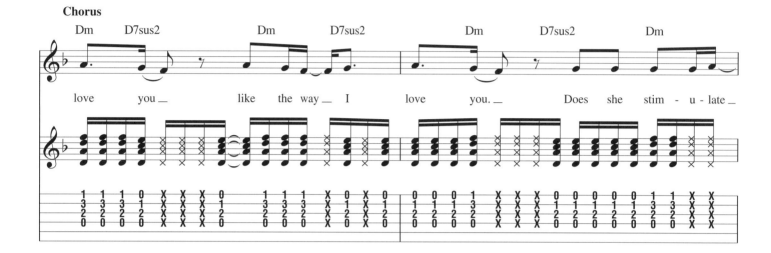

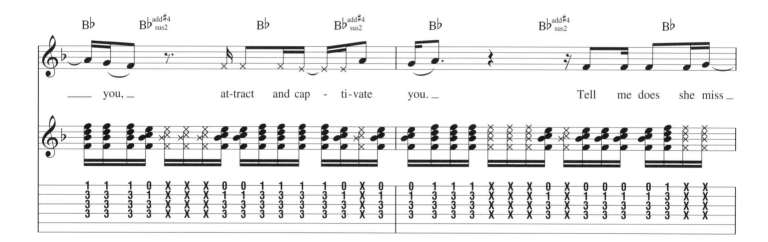

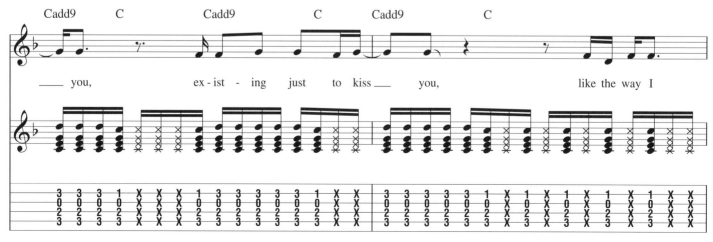

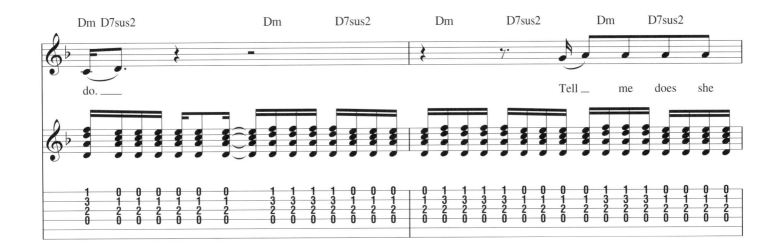

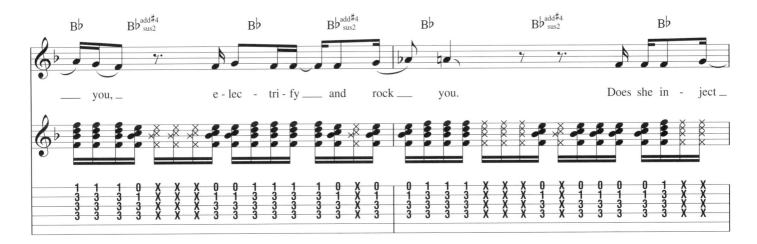

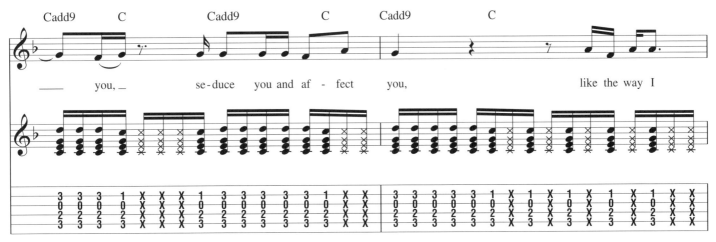

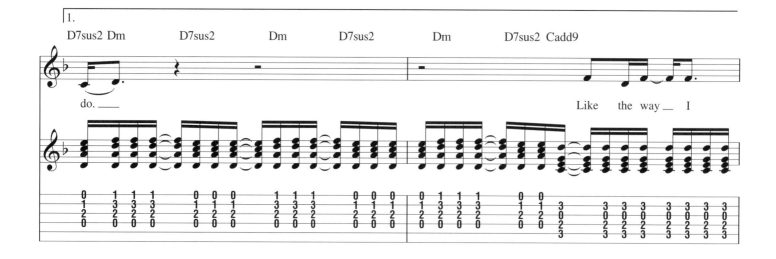

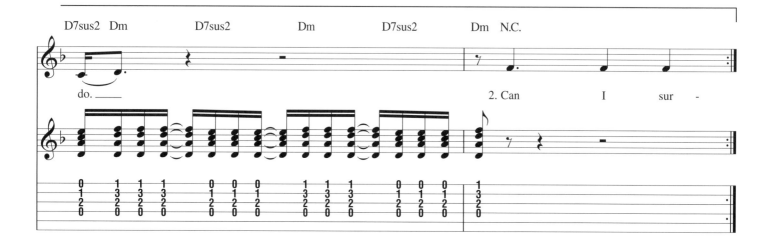

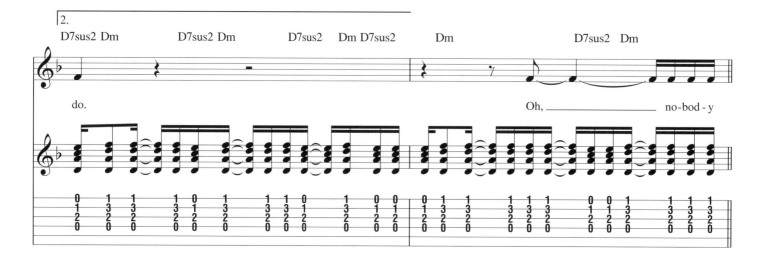

Bridge

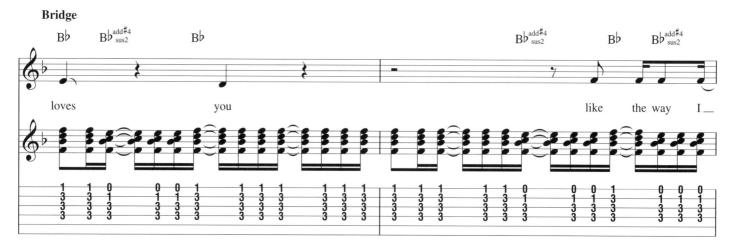

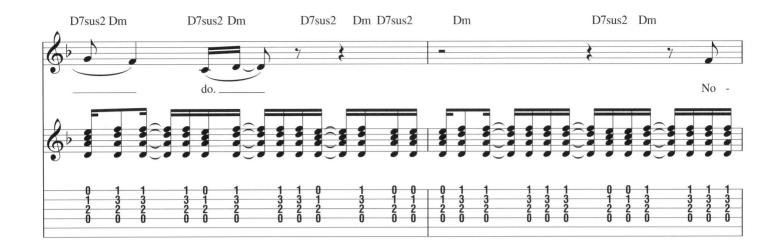

do. _____ No -

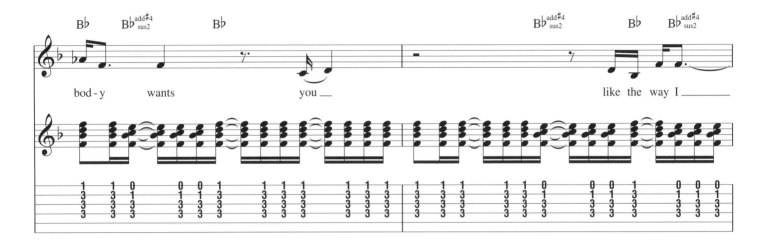

bod - y   wants   you ___   like the way I _____

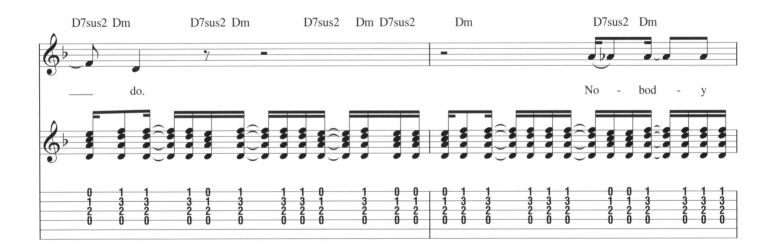

____ do.   No - bod - y

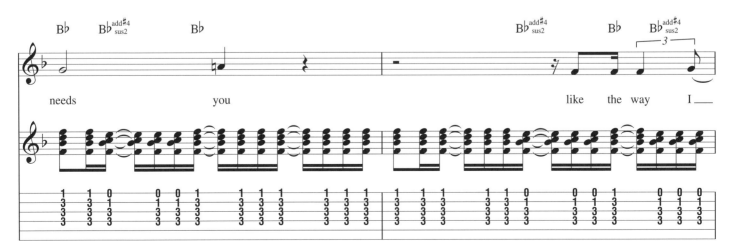

needs   you   like   the   way   I ___

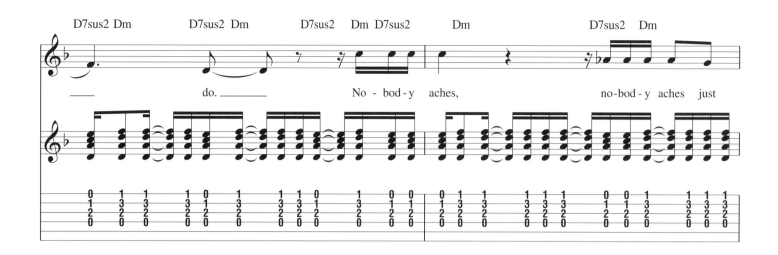

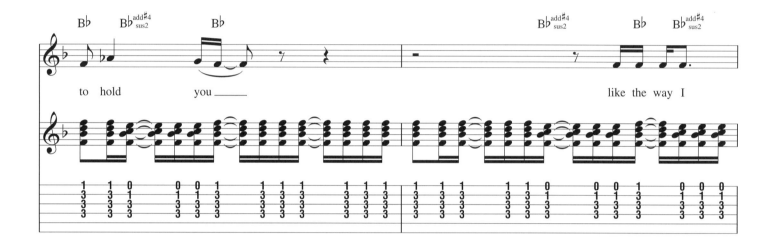

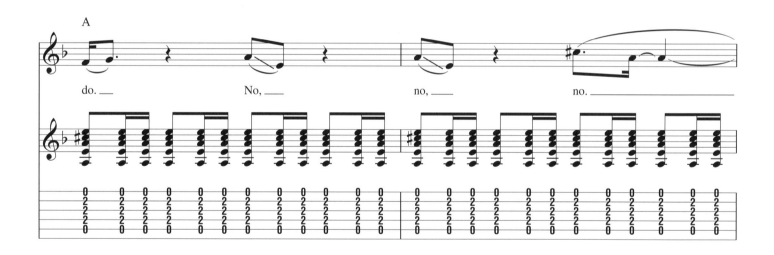

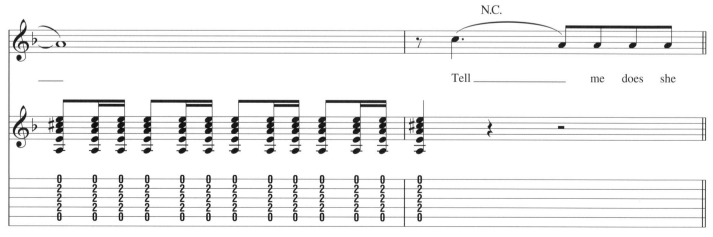

Chorus

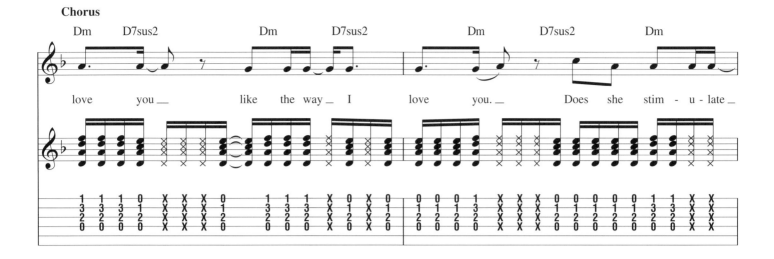

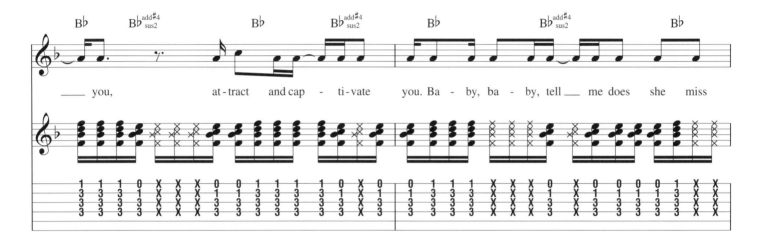

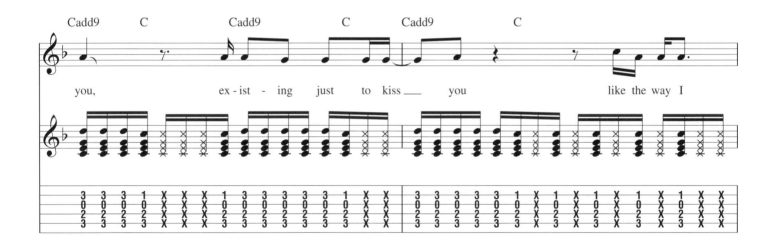

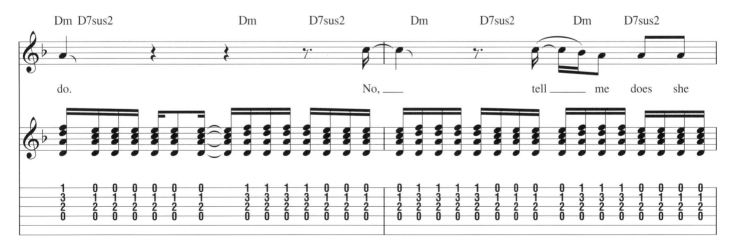

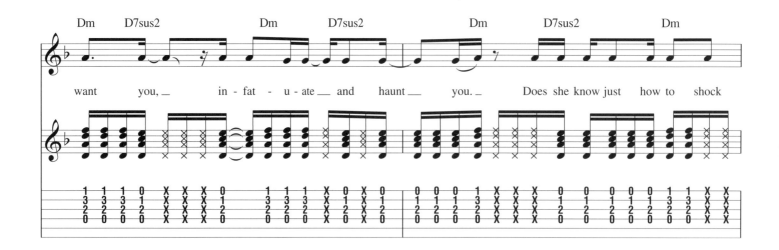

want you, __ in-fat-u-ate __ and haunt __ you. __ Does she know just how to shock

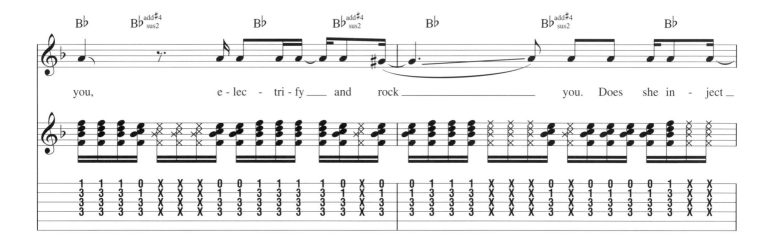

you, e-lec-tri-fy __ and rock _____ you. Does she in-ject __

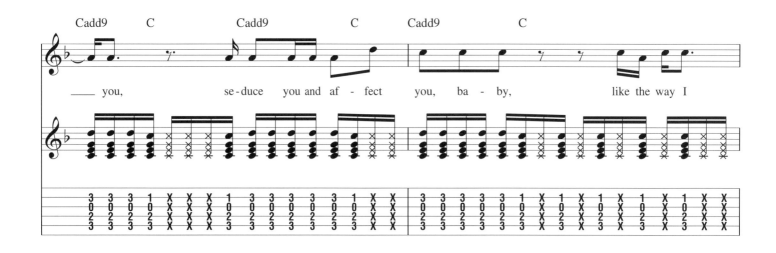

__ you, se-duce you and af-fect you, ba-by, like the way I

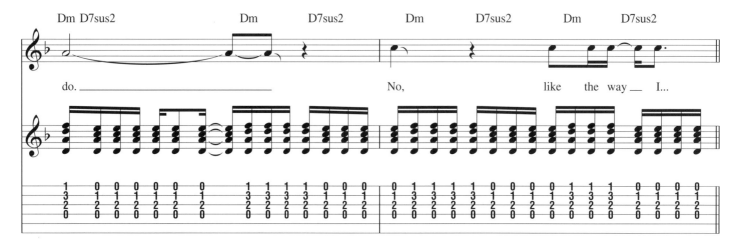

do. _____ No, like the way __ I...

Outro
w/ Voc. ad lib.

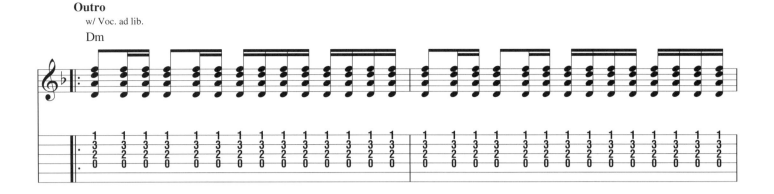

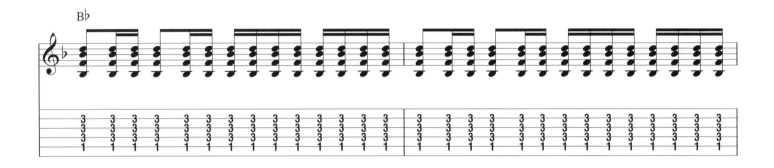

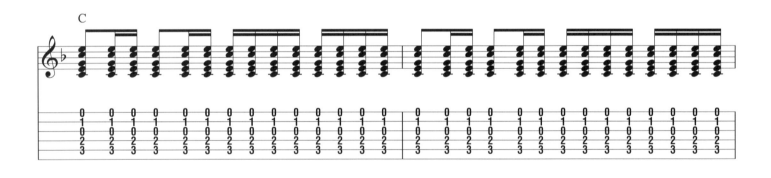

Repeat and fade

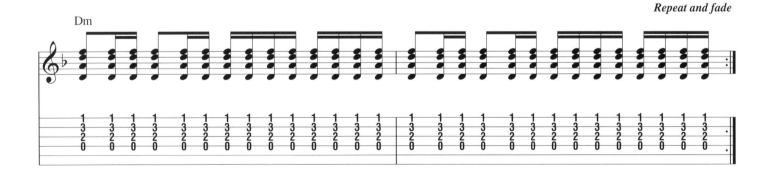

Additional Lyrics

2. Can I survive all the implications?
   Even if I tried could you be less than an addiction?
   Don't you think I know there's so many others
   Who would beg, steal and lie and fight, kill, and die,
   Just to hold you, hold you, like I do?

Stay

Words and Music by Lisa Loeb

Capo VI

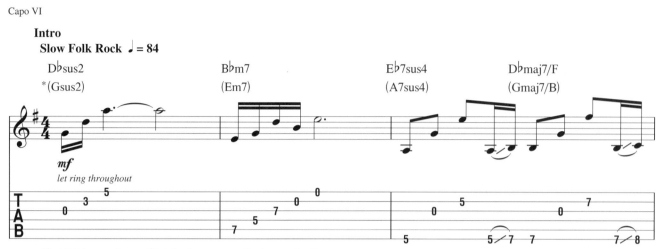

*Symbols in parentheses reflect chord names respective to capoed guitar.
Symbols above reflect actual sounding chords. Capoed fret is "0" in tab.

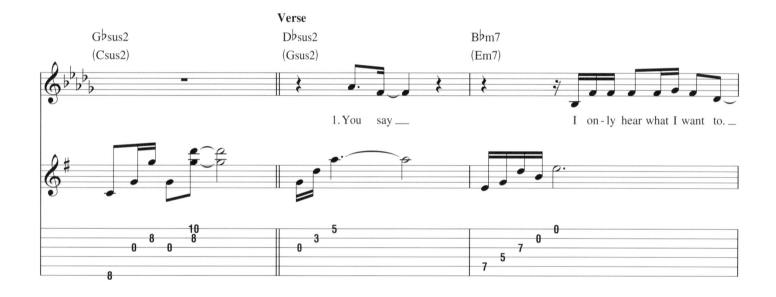

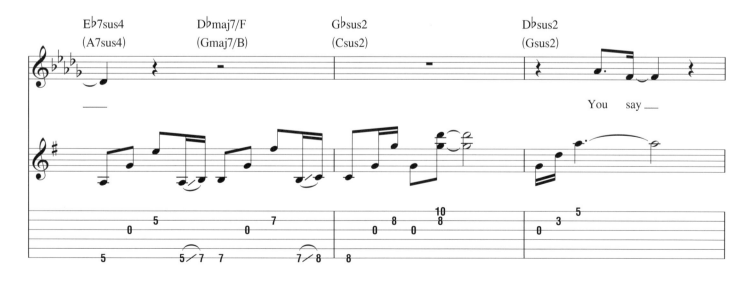

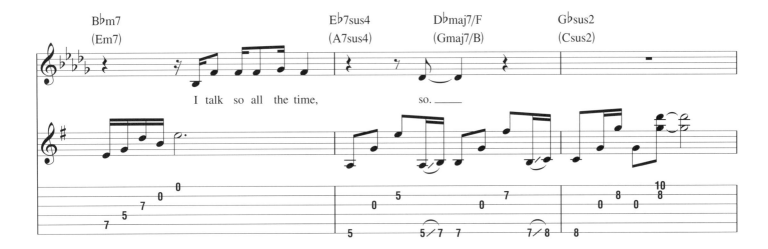

I talk so all the time, so. _____

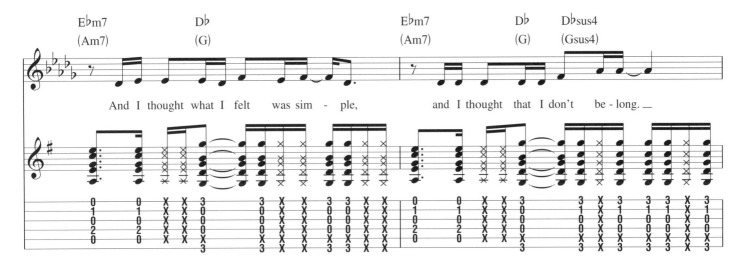

And I thought what I felt was sim-ple, and I thought that I don't be-long. _____

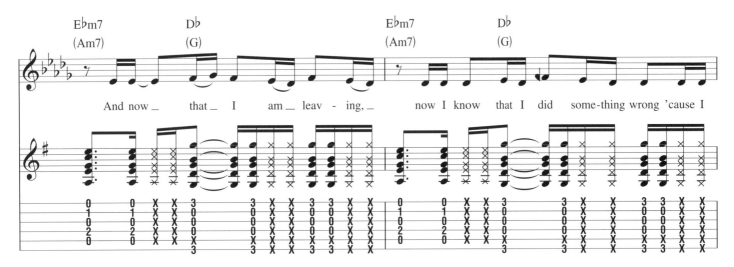

And now _____ that _____ I am _____ leav-ing, _____ now I know that I did some-thing wrong 'cause I

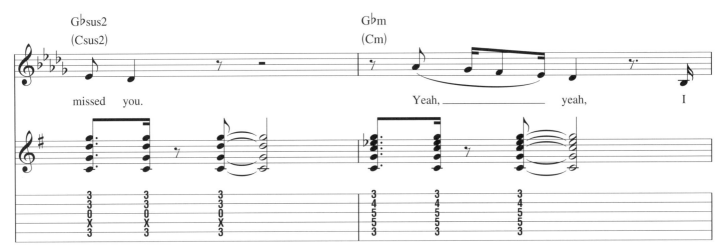

missed you. Yeah, _____ yeah, I

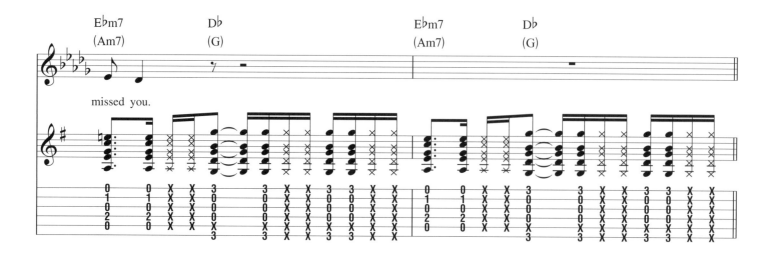

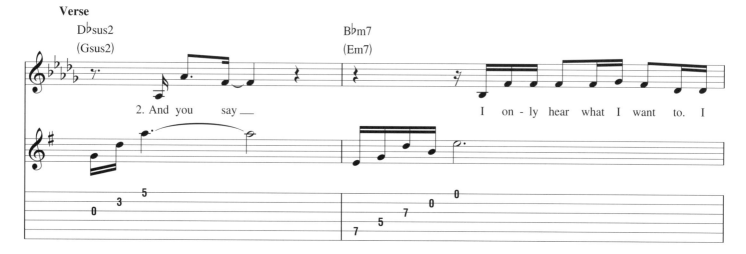

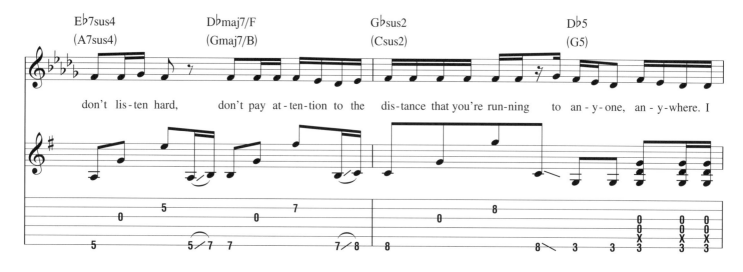

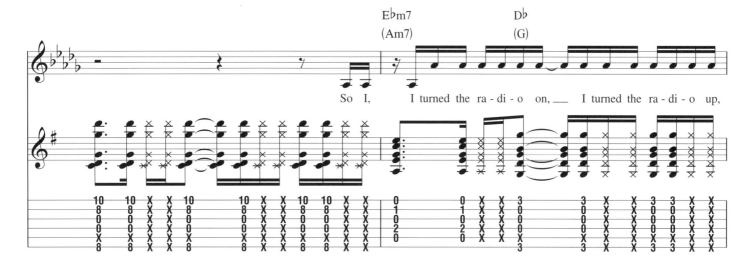

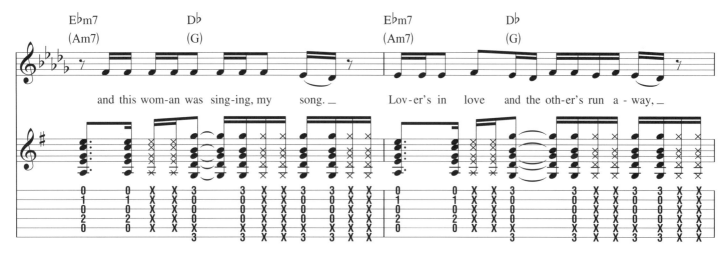

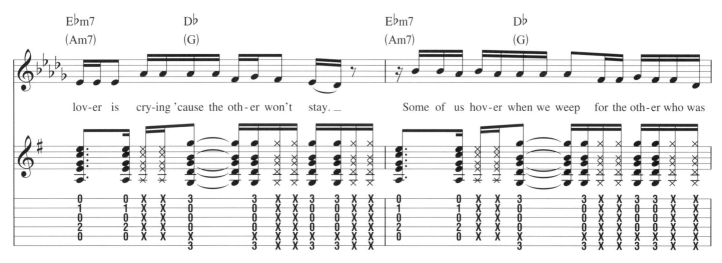

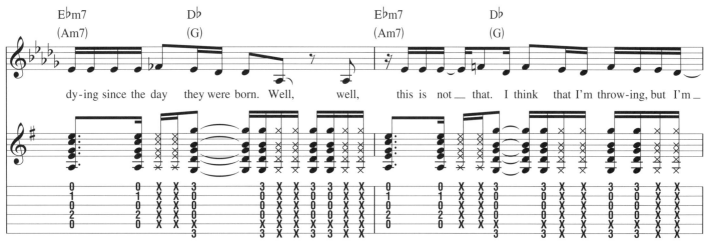

thrown. ___ And I thought I'd live for-ev-er, but now I'm not so sure. You try to

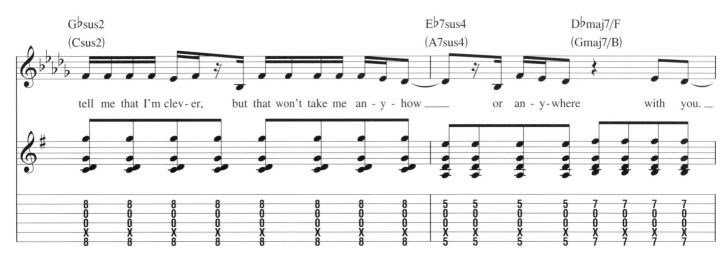

tell me that I'm clev-er, but that won't take me an-y-how ___ or an-y-where with you. _

Verse

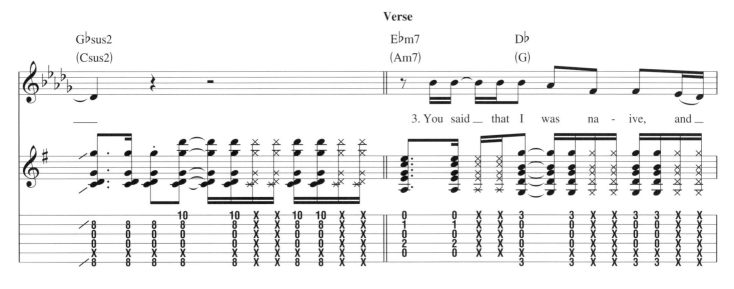

3. You said _ that I was na-ive, and _

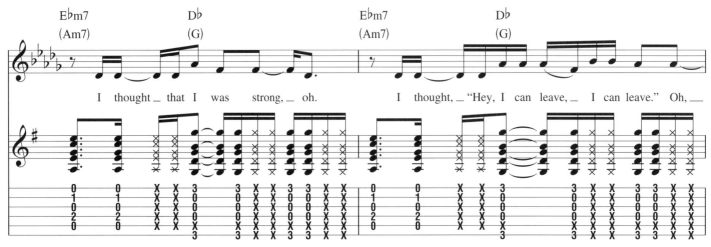

I thought _ that I was strong, _ oh. I thought, "Hey, I can leave, _ I can leave." Oh, _

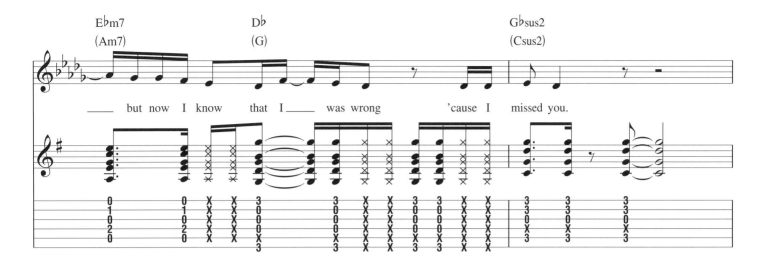

but now I know that I ___ was wrong ___ 'cause I ___ missed you.

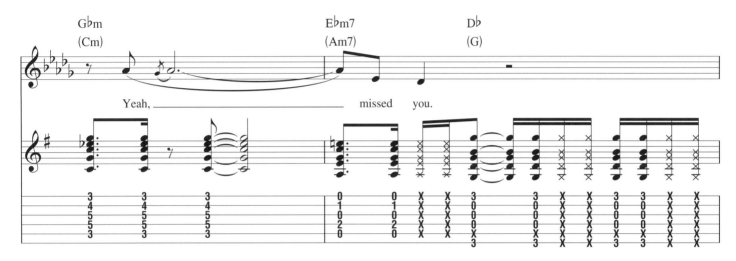

Yeah, _____ missed you.

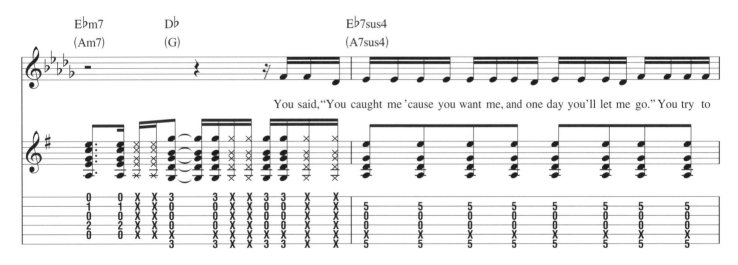

You said, "You caught me 'cause you want me, and one day you'll let me go." You try to

give a-way a keep-er ___ or keep me 'cause you know you're just so ___ scared ___ to lose. _____

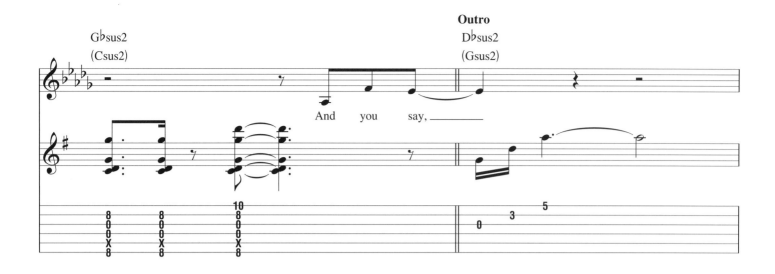

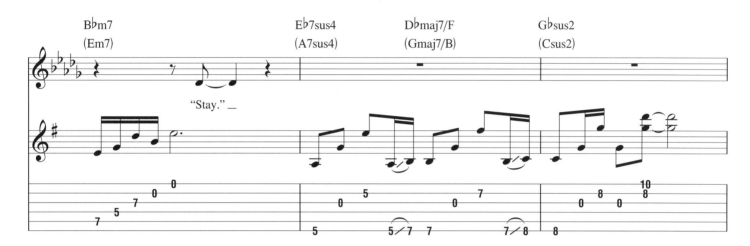

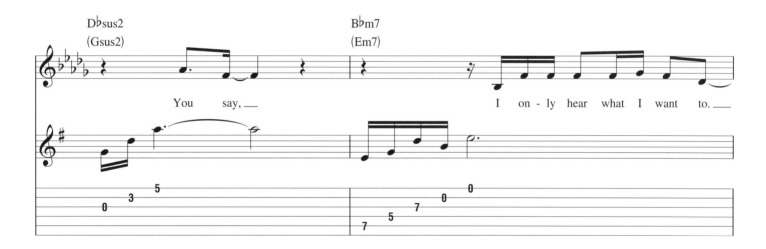

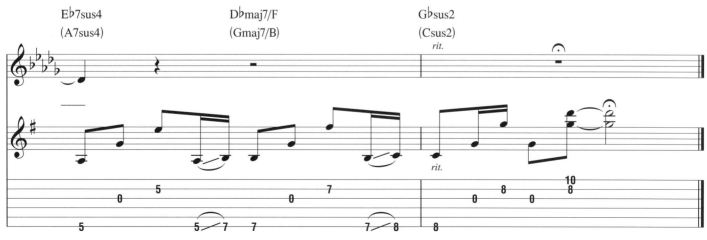

You Were Meant for Me

Lyrics by Jewel Kilcher
Music by Jewel Kilcher and Steve Poltz

Tune down 1/2 step:
(low to high) E♭-A♭-D♭-G♭-B♭-E♭

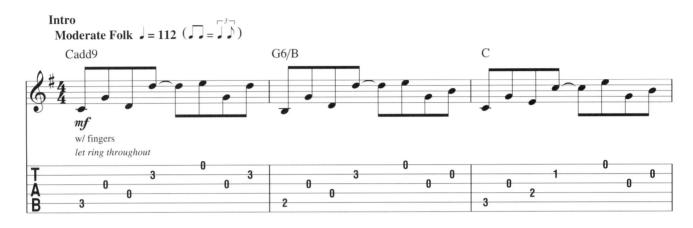

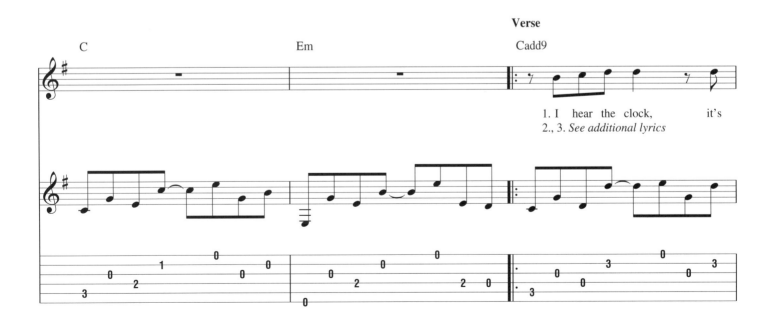

1. I hear the clock,   it's
2., 3. *See additional lyrics*

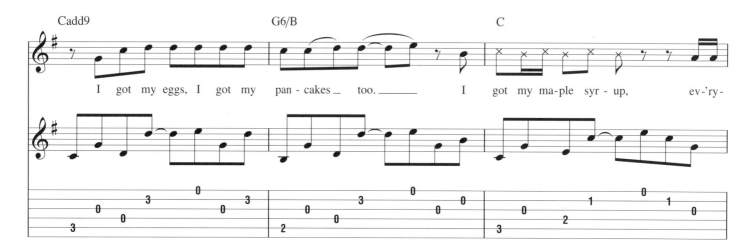

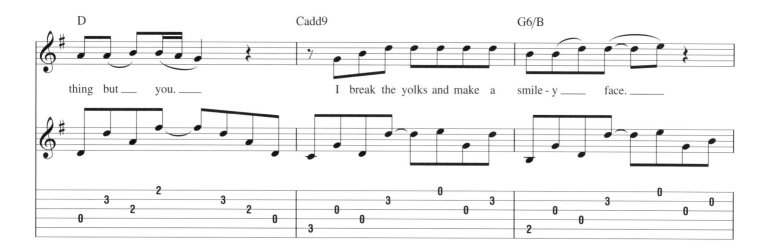

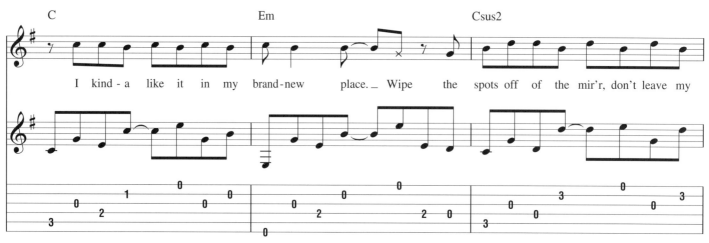

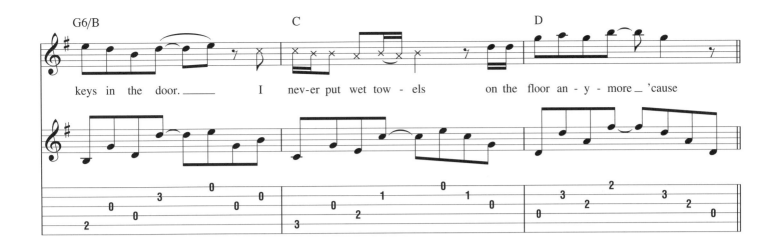

keys in the door._____ I nev-er put wet tow - els   on the floor an - y - more __ 'cause

Chorus

dreams __ last __   so __ long, __   e - ven af - ter you're gone. __

_____   I   know __   that you love __ me __   and __

soon _____ you __ will see _____   you were meant for   me ___   and

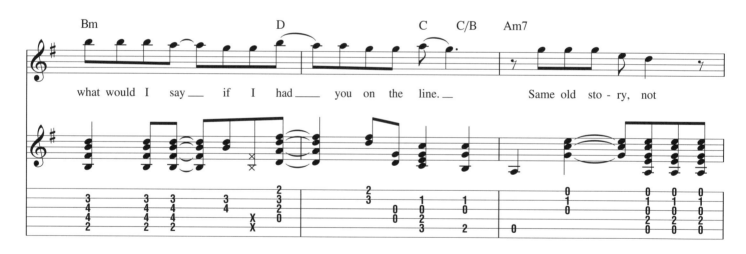

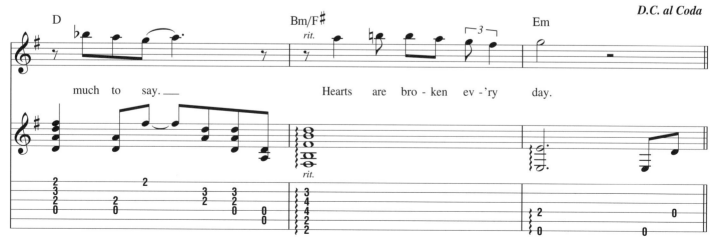

⊕ Coda

you.   Yeah,   you were

Outro

meant for   me ___   and   I   was meant for ___   you. ___

Additional Lyrics

2. I called my momma, she was out for a walk.
   Consoled a cup of coffee but it didn't wanna talk.
   So I picked up the paper, it was more bad news;
   More hearts being broken or people being used.
   Put on my coat in the pouring rain.
   I saw a movie, it just wasn't the same
   'Cause it was happy, oh, I was sad
   And it made me miss you, oh, so bad 'cause...

3. I brush my teeth, I put the cap back on.
   I know you hate it when I leave the light on.
   I pick a book up and then I turn the sheets down
   And then I take a deep breath and a good look around.
   Put on my PJs and hop into bed.
   I'm half alive but I feel mostly dead.
   I try and tell myself it'll all be alright.
   I just shouldn't think anymore tonight 'cause...

Torn

Words and Music by Phil Thornalley, Scott Cutler and Anne Previn

Capo V

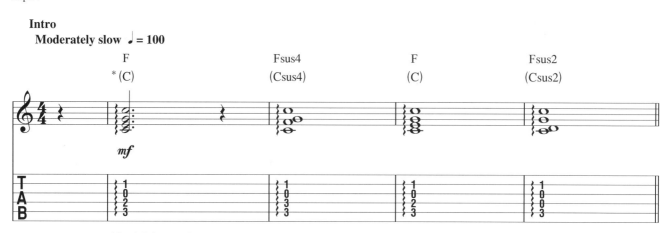

*Symbols in parentheses represent chord names respective to capoed guitar.
Symbols above reflect actual sounding chords. Capoed fret is "0" in tab.

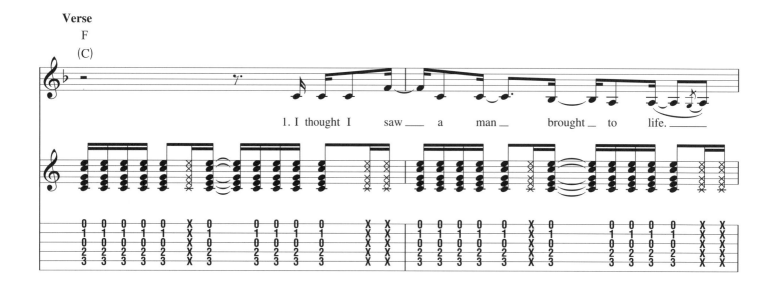

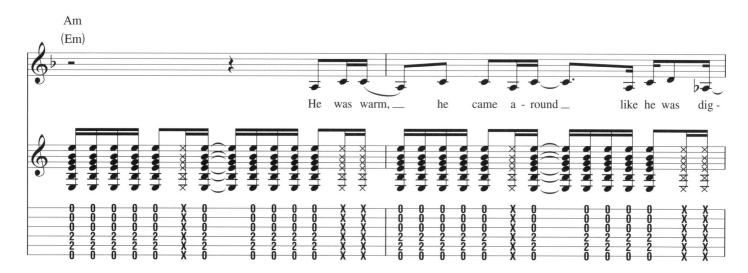

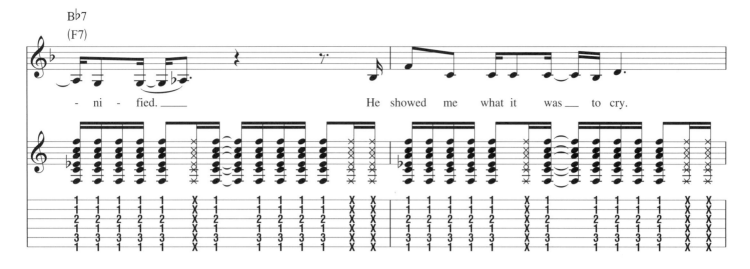

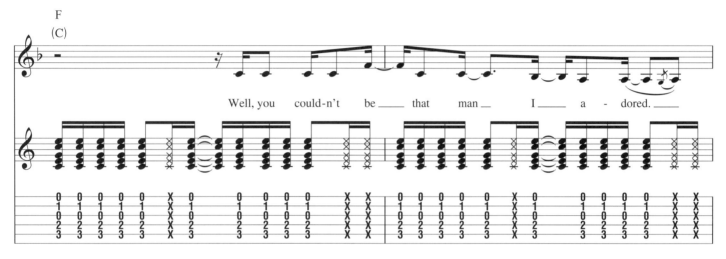

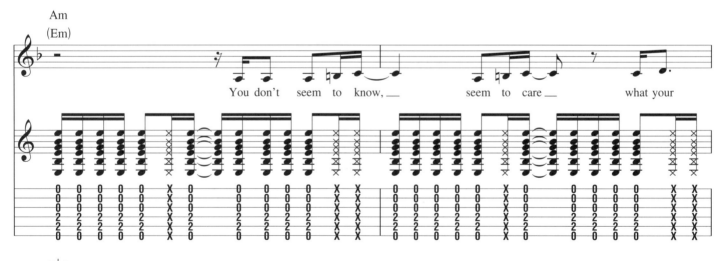

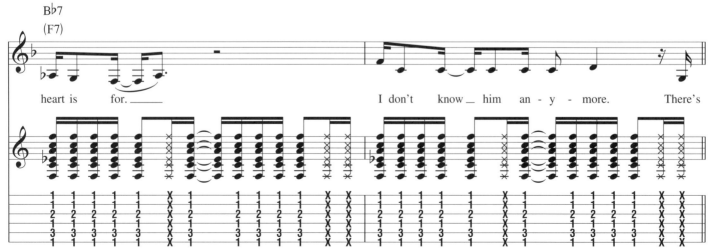

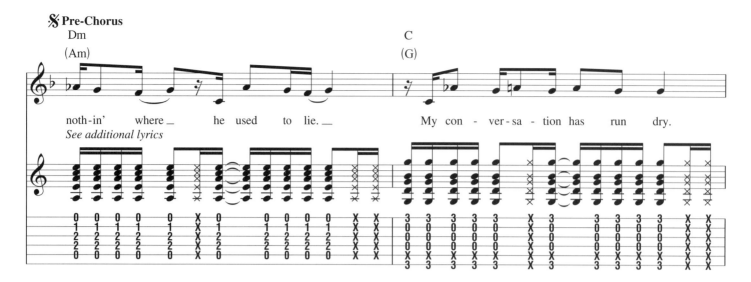

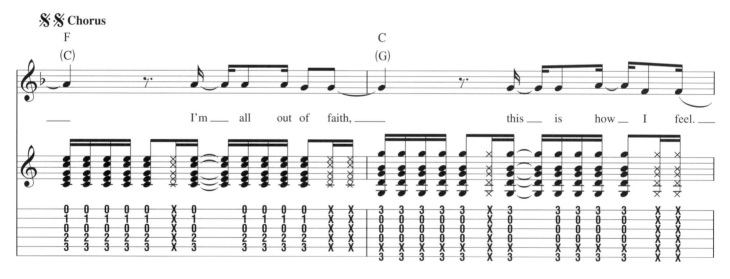

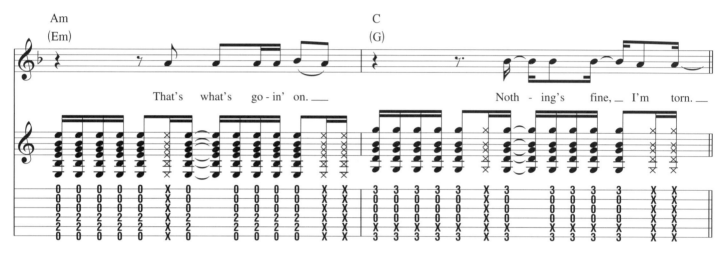

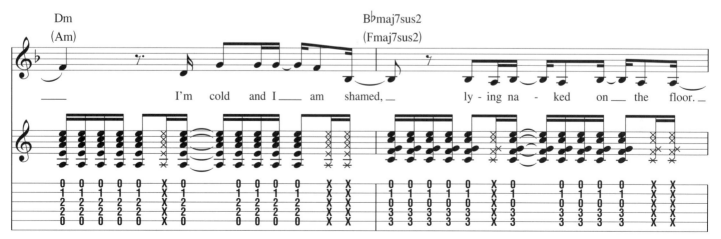

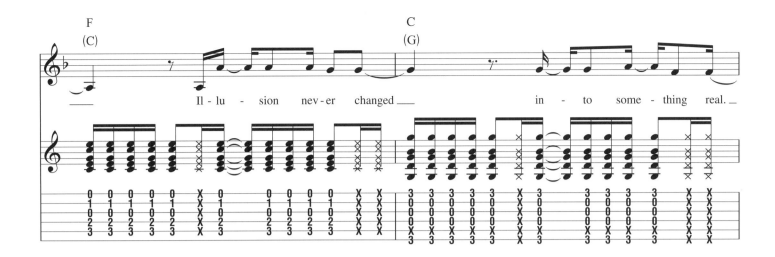

Il-lu - sion nev-er changed ___ in - to some-thing real. ___

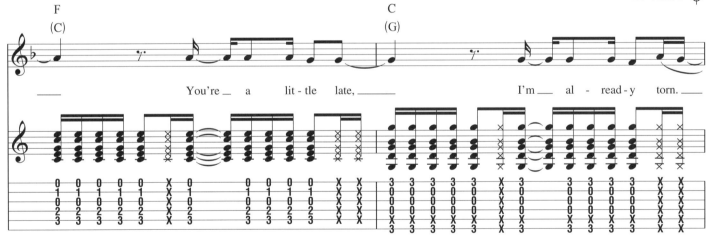

To Coda 2 ⊕

I'm wide a - wake ___ and I ___ can see ___ the per - fect sky ___ is torn. ___

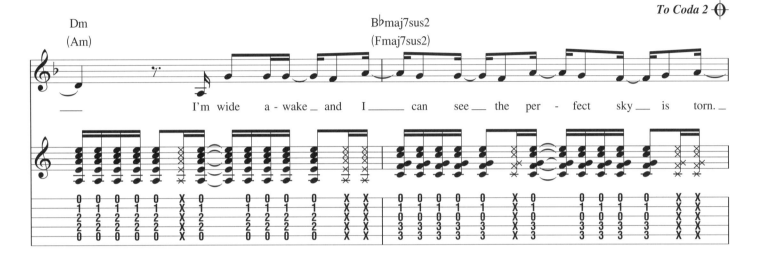

To Coda 1

You're ___ a lit - tle late, ___ I'm ___ al - read-y torn. ___

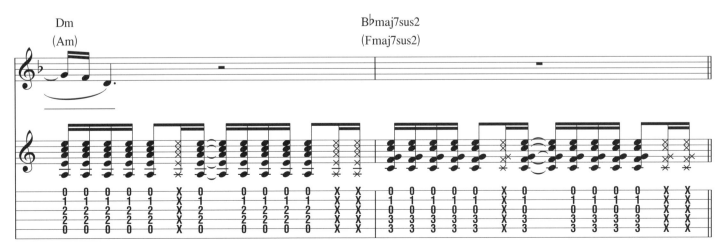

Verse

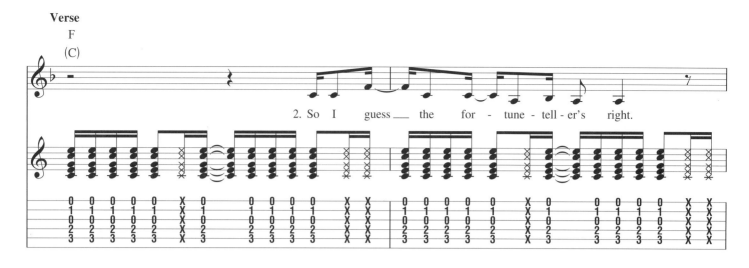

2. So I guess ___ the for - tune - tell - er's right.

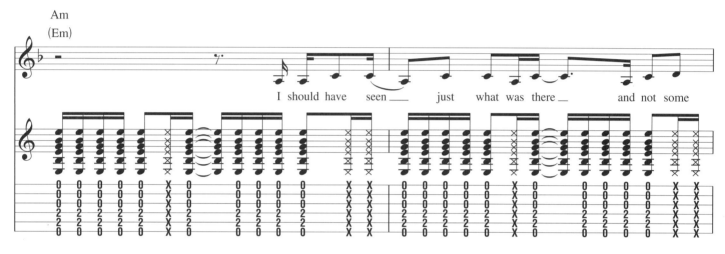

I should have seen ___ just what was there ___ and not some

D.S. al Coda 1

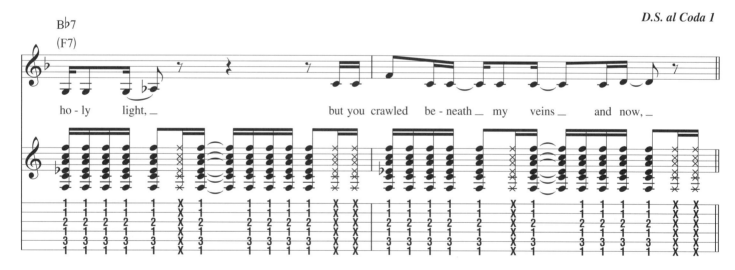

ho - ly light, ___ but you crawled be - neath ___ my veins ___ and now, ___

Coda 1

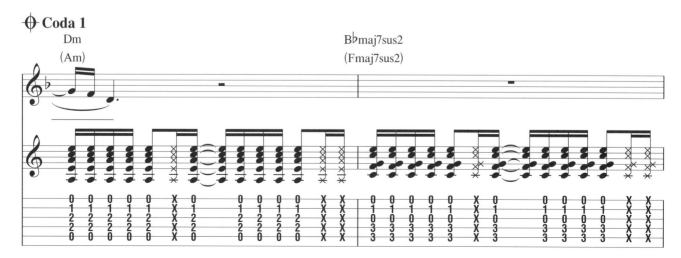

66

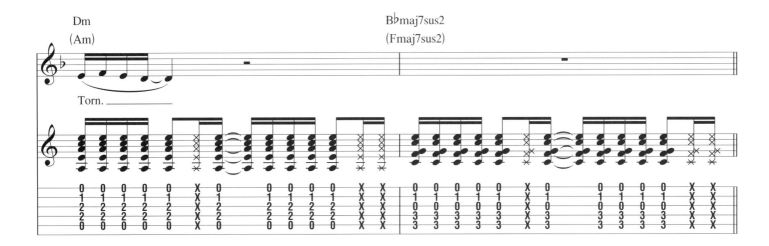

Torn.

Interlude

(Oo, _____ oo.) _____

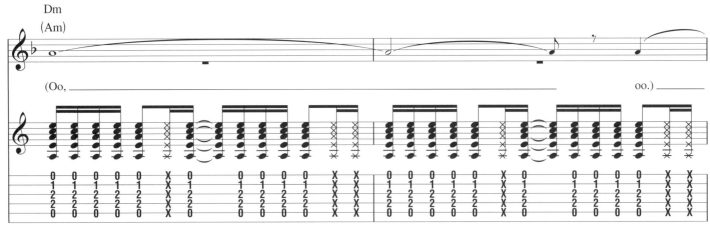

There's

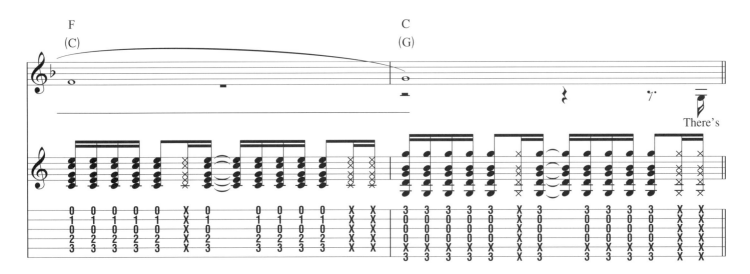

Pre-Chorus

noth-ing where ___ he used to lie. ___ My in - spi - ra - tion has run dry.

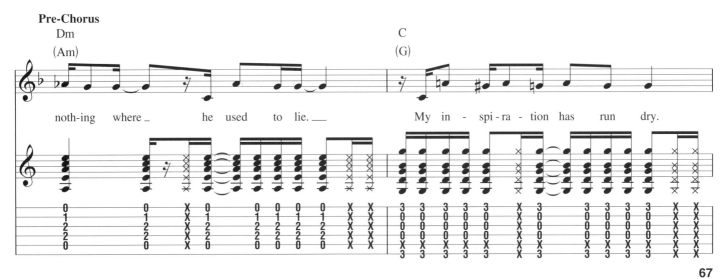

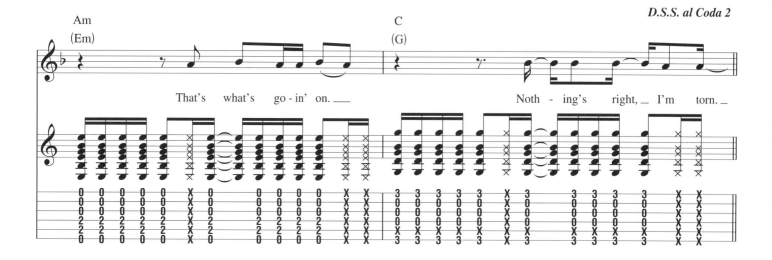

That's what's go-in' on. ___ Noth - ing's right, ___ I'm torn. ___

⊕ Coda 2

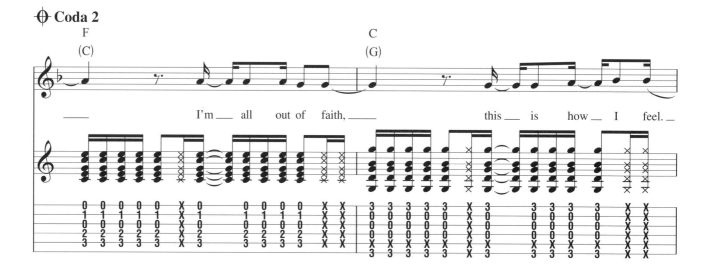

___ I'm ___ all out of faith, ___ this ___ is how ___ I feel. ___

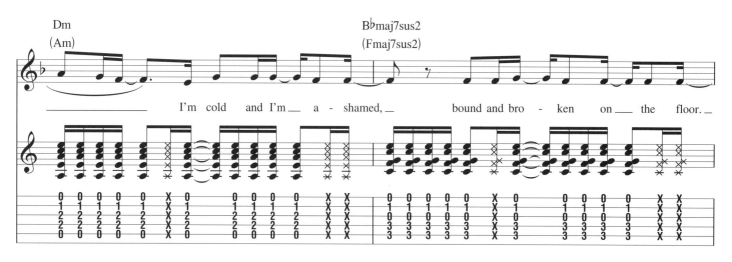

___ I'm cold and I'm ___ a - shamed, ___ bound and bro - ken on ___ the floor. ___

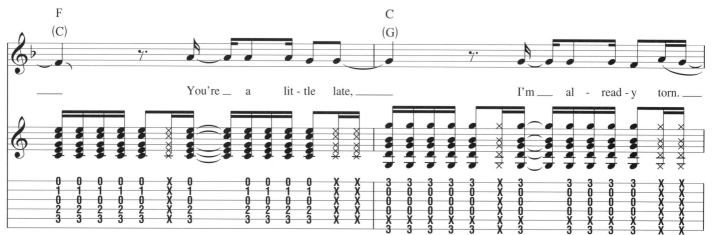

___ You're ___ a lit - tle late, ___ I'm ___ al - read - y torn. ___

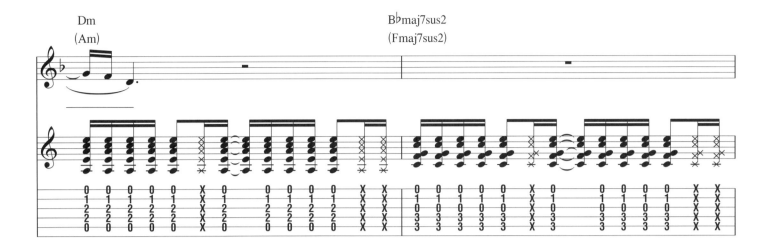

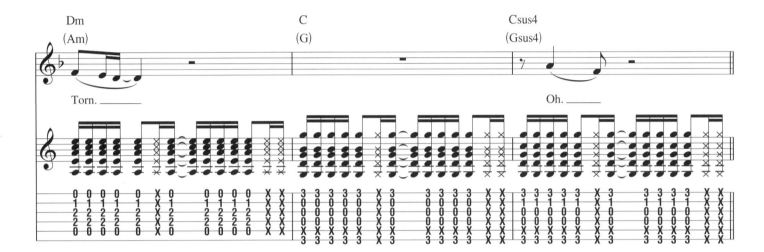

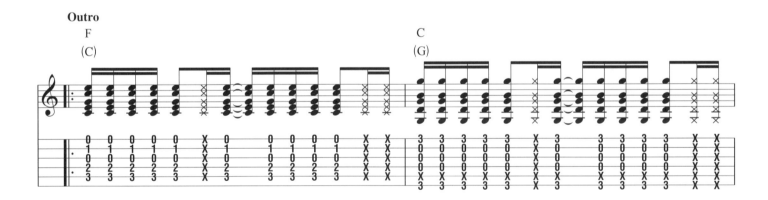

Repeat and fade

Additional Lyrics

Pre-Chorus I don't care, I have no luck.
I don't miss it all that much.
There's just so many things
That I can't touch. I'm torn.

HAL•LEONARD GUITAR PLAY-ALONG®

This series will help you play your favorite songs quickly and easily. Just follow the tab and listen to the CD to hear how the guitar should sound, and then play along using the separate backing tracks. Mac or PC users can also slow down the tempo without changing pitch by using the CD in their computer. The melody and lyrics are included in the book so that you can sing or simply follow along.

1. ROCK
Day Tripper • Message in a Bottle • Refugee • Shattered • Sunshine of Your Love • Takin' Care of Business • Tush • Walk This Way.
00699570 ....$16.99

2. ACOUSTIC
Angie • Behind Blue Eyes • Best of My Love • Blackbird • Dust in the Wind • Layla • Night Moves • Yesterday.
00699569..$16.95

3. HARD ROCK
Crazy Train • Iron Man • Living After Midnight • Rock You like a Hurricane • Round and Round • Smoke on the Water • Sweet Child o' Mine • You Really Got Me.
00699573..$16.95

4. POP/ROCK
Breakdown • Crazy Little Thing Called Love • Hit Me with Your Best Shot • I Want You to Want Me • Lights • R.O.C.K. in the U.S.A. • Summer of '69 • What I Like About You.
00699571..$16.99

5. MODERN ROCK
Aerials • Alive • Bother • Chop Suey! • Control • Last Resort • Take a Look Around (Theme from *M:I-2*) • Wish You Were Here.
00699574 ....$16.99

6. '90s ROCK
Are You Gonna Go My Way • Come out and Play • I'll Stick Around • Know Your Enemy • Man in the Box • Outshined • Smells like Teen Spirit • Under the Bridge.
00699572..$16.99

7. BLUES
All Your Love (I Miss Loving) • Born Under a Bad Sign • Hide Away • I'm Tore Down • I'm Your Hoochie Coochie Man • Pride and Joy • Sweet Home Chicago • The Thrill Is Gone.
00699575..$16.95

8. ROCK
All Right Now • Black Magic Woman • Get Back • Hey Joe • Layla • Love Me Two Times • Won't Get Fooled Again • You Really Got Me.
00699585..$14.95

9. PUNK ROCK
All the Small Things • Fat Lip • Flavor of the Weak • I Feel So • Lifestyles of the Rich and Famous • Say It Ain't So • Self Esteem • (So) Tired of Waiting for You.
00699576..$14.95

10. ACOUSTIC
Here Comes the Sun • Landslide • The Magic Bus • Norwegian Wood (This Bird Has Flown) • Pink Houses • Space Oddity • Tangled Up in Blue • Tears in Heaven.
00699586..$16.95

11. EARLY ROCK
Fun, Fun, Fun • Hound Dog • Louie, Louie • No Particular Place to Go • Oh, Pretty Woman • Rock Around the Clock • Under the Boardwalk • Wild Thing.
0699579..$14.95

12. POP/ROCK
867-5309/Jenny • Every Breath You Take • Money for Nothing • Rebel, Rebel • Run to You • Ticket to Ride • Wonderful Tonight • You Give Love a Bad Name.
00699587..$14.95

13. FOLK ROCK
Annie's Song • Leaving on a Jet Plane • Suite: Judy Blue Eyes • This Land Is Your Land • Time in a Bottle • Turn! Turn! Turn! • You've Got a Friend • You've Got to Hide Your Love Away.
00699581..$14.95

14. BLUES ROCK
Blue on Black • Crossfire • Cross Road Blues (Crossroads) • The House Is Rockin' • La Grange • Move It on Over • Roadhouse Blues • Statesboro Blues.
00699582..$16.95

15. R&B
Ain't Too Proud to Beg • Brick House • Get Ready • I Can't Help Myself • I Got You (I Feel Good) • I Heard It Through the Grapevine • My Girl • Shining Star.
00699583..$14.95

16. JAZZ
All Blues • Bluesette • Footprints • How Insensitive • Misty • Satin Doll • Stella by Starlight • Tenor Madness.
00699584..$15.95

17. COUNTRY
Amie • Boot Scootin' Boogie • Chattahoochee • Folsom Prison Blues • Friends in Low Places • Forever and Ever, Amen • T-R-O-U-B-L-E • Workin' Man Blues.
00699588..$15.95

18. ACOUSTIC ROCK
About a Girl • Breaking the Girl • Drive • Iris • More than Words • Patience • Silent Lucidity • 3 AM.
00699577..$15.95

19. SOUL
Get Up (I Feel like Being) a Sex Machine • Green Onions • In the Midnight Hour • Knock on Wood • Mustang Sally • Respect • (Sittin' On) The Dock of the Bay • Soul Man.
00699578..$14.95

20. ROCKABILLY
Be-Bop-A-Lula • Blue Suede Shoes • Hello Mary Lou • Little Sister • Mystery Train • Rock This Town • Stray Cat Strut • That'll Be the Day.
00699580..$14.95

21. YULETIDE
Angels We Have Heard on High • Away in a Manger • Deck the Hall • The First Noel • Go, Tell It on the Mountain • Jingle Bells • Joy to the World • O Little Town of Bethlehem.
00699602..$14.95

22. CHRISTMAS
The Christmas Song • Frosty the Snow Man • Happy Xmas • Here Comes Santa Claus • Jingle-Bell Rock • Merry Christmas, Darling • Rudolph the Red-Nosed Reindeer • Silver Bells.
00699600..$15.95

23. SURF
Let's Go Trippin' • Out of Limits • Penetration • Pipeline • Surf City • Surfin' U.S.A. • Walk Don't Run • The Wedge.
00699635..$14.95

24. ERIC CLAPTON
Badge • Bell Bottom Blues • Change the World • Cocaine • Key to the Highway • Lay Down Sally • White Room • Wonderful Tonight.
00699649..$16.95

25. LENNON & McCARTNEY
Back in the U.S.S.R. • Drive My Car • Get Back • A Hard Day's Night • I Feel Fine • Paperback Writer • Revolution • Ticket to Ride.
00699642 ....$14.95

26. ELVIS PRESLEY
All Shook Up • Blue Suede Shoes • Don't Be Cruel • Heartbreak Hotel • Hound Dog • Jailhouse Rock • Little Sister • Mystery Train.
00699643..$14.95

27. DAVID LEE ROTH
Ain't Talkin' 'bout Love • Dance the Night Away • Hot for Teacher • Just like Paradise • A Lil' Ain't Enough • Runnin' with the Devil • Unchained • Yankee Rose.
00699645..$16.95

28. GREG KOCH
Chief's Blues • Death of a Bassman • Dylan the Villain • The Grip • Holy Grail • Spank It • Tonus Diabolicus • Zoiks.
00699646..$14.95

29. BOB SEGER
Against the Wind • Betty Lou's Gettin' out Tonight • Hollywood Nights • Mainstreet • Night Moves • Old Time Rock & Roll • Rock and Roll Never Forgets • Still the Same.
00699647..$14.95

30. KISS
Cold Gin • Detroit Rock City • Deuce • Firehouse • Heaven's on Fire • Love Gun • Rock and Roll All Nite • Shock Me.
00699644..$14.95

31. CHRISTMAS HITS
Blue Christmas • Do You Hear What I Hear • Happy Holiday • I Saw Mommy Kissing Santa Claus • I'll Be Home for Christmas • Let It Snow! Let It Snow! Let It Snow! • Little Saint Nick • Snowfall.
00699652..$14.95

32. THE OFFSPRING
Bad Habit • Come out and Play • Gone Away • Gotta Get Away • Hit That • The Kids Aren't Alright • Pretty Fly (For a White Guy) • Self Esteem.
00699653..$14.95

33. ACOUSTIC CLASSICS
Across the Universe • Babe, I'm Gonna Leave You • Crazy on You • Heart of Gold • Hotel California • I'd Love to Change the World • Thick as a Brick • Wanted Dead or Alive.
00699656..$16.95

34. CLASSIC ROCK
Aqualung • Born to Be Wild • The Boys Are Back in Town • Brown Eyed Girl • Reeling in the Years • Rock'n Me • Rocky Mountain Way • Sweet Emotion.
00699658..$16.95

35. HAIR METAL
Decadence Dance • Don't Treat Me Bad • Down Boys • Seventeen • Shake Me • Up All Night • Wait • Talk Dirty to Me.
00699660..$16.95

36. SOUTHERN ROCK
Can't You See • Flirtin' with Disaster • Hold on Loosely • Jessica • Mississippi Queen • Ramblin' Man • Sweet Home Alabama • What's Your Name.
00699661..$16.95

37. ACOUSTIC METAL
Every Rose Has Its Thorn • Fly to the Angels • Hole Hearted • Love Is on the Way • Love of a Lifetime • Signs • To Be with You • When the Children Cry.
00699662..$16.95

38. BLUES
Boom Boom • Cold Shot • Crosscut Saw • Everyday I Have the Blues • Frosty • Further on up the Road • Killing Floor • Texas Flood.
00699663..$16.95

39. '80s METAL
Bark at the Moon • Big City Nights • Breaking the Chains • Cult of Personality • Lay It Down • Living on a Prayer • Panama • Smokin' in the Boys Room.
00699664..$16.99

40. INCUBUS
Are You In? • Drive • Megalomaniac • Nice to Know You • Pardon Me • Stellar • Talk Shows on Mute • Wish You Were Here.
00699668..$17.95

41. ERIC CLAPTON
After Midnight • Can't Find My Way Home • Forever Man • I Shot the Sheriff • I'm Tore Down • Pretending • Running on Faith • Tears in Heaven.
00699669..$16.95

42. CHART HITS
Are You Gonna Be My Girl • Heaven • Here Without You • I Believe in a Thing Called Love • Just like You • Last Train Home • This Love • Until the Day I Die.
00699670..$16.95

43. LYNYRD SKYNYRD
Don't Ask Me No Questions • Free Bird • Gimme Three Steps • I Know a Little • Saturday Night Special • Sweet Home Alabama • That Smell • You Got That Right.
00699681..$17.95

44. JAZZ
I Remember You • I'll Remember April • Impressions • In a Mellow Tone • Moonlight in Vermont • On a Slow Boat to China • Things Ain't What They Used to Be • Yesterdays.
00699689..$14.95

45. TV THEMES
Themes from shows such as: The Addams Family • Hawaii Five-O • King of the Hill • Charlie Brown • Mission: Impossible • The Munsters • The Simpsons • Star Trek®.
00699718..$14.95

46. MAINSTREAM ROCK
Just a Girl • Keep Away • Kryptonite • Lightning Crashes • 1979 • One Step Closer • Scar Tissue • Torn.
00699722..$16.95

47. HENDRIX SMASH HITS
All Along the Watchtower • Can You See Me? • Crosstown Traffic • Fire • Foxey Lady • Hey Joe • Manic Depression • Purple Haze • Red House • Remember • Stone Free • The Wind Cries Mary.
00699723..$19.95

48. AEROSMITH CLASSICS
Back in the Saddle • Draw the Line • Dream On • Last Child • Mama Kin • Same Old Song & Dance • Sweet Emotion • Walk This Way.
00699724..$16.99

49. STEVIE RAY VAUGHAN
Couldn't Stand the Weather • Empty Arms • Lenny • Little Wing • Look at Little Sister • Love Struck Baby • The Sky Is Crying • Tightrope.
00699725..$16.95

50. NÜ METAL
Duality • Here to Stay • In the End • Judith • Nookie • So Cold • Toxicity • Whatever.
00699726..$14.95

51. ALTERNATIVE '90s
Alive • Cherub Rock • Come As You Are • Give It Away • Jane Says • No Excuses • No Rain • Santeria.
00699727..$12.95

52. FUNK
Cissy Strut • Flashlight • Funk #49 • I Just Want to Celebrate • It's Your Thing • Le Freak • Papa's Got a Brand New Bag • Pick up the Pieces.
00699728..$14.95

54. HEAVY METAL
Am I Evil? • Back in Black • Holy Diver • Lights Out • The Trooper • You've Got Another Thing Comin' • The Zoo.
00699730..$14.95

55. POP METAL
Beautiful Girls • Cherry Pie • Get the Funk Out • Here I Go Again • Nothin' but a Good Time • Photograph • Turn up the Radio • We're Not Gonna Take It.
00699731..$14.95

56. FOO FIGHTERS
All My Life • Best of You • DOA • I'll Stick Around • Learn to Fly • Monkey Wrench • My Hero • This Is a Call.
00699749..$14.95

57. SYSTEM OF A DOWN
Aerials • B.Y.O.B. • Chop Suey! • Innervision • Question! • Spiders • Sugar • Toxicity.
00699751..$14.95

58. BLINK-182
Adam's Song • All the Small Things • Dammit • Feeling This • Man Overboard • The Rock Show • Stay Together for the Kids • What's My Age Again?
00699772..$14.95

59. GODSMACK
Awake • Bad Religion • Greed • I Stand Alone • Keep Away • Running Blind • Straight out of Line • Whatever.
00699773..$14.95

60. 3 DOORS DOWN
Away from the Sun • Duck and Run • Here Without You • Kryptonite • Let Me Go • Live for Today • Loser • When I'm Gone.
00699774..$14.95

61. SLIPKNOT
Before I Forget • Duality • The Heretic Anthem • Left Behind • My Plague • Spit It Out • Vermilion • Wait and Bleed.
00699775..$14.95

62. CHRISTMAS CAROLS
God Rest Ye Merry, Gentlemen • Hark! The Herald Angels Sing • It Came upon the Midnight Clear • O Come, All Ye Faithful (Adeste Fideles) • O Holy Night • Silent Night • We Three Kings of Orient Are • What Child Is This?
00699798..$12.95

63. CREEDENCE CLEARWATER REVIVAL
Bad Moon Rising • Born on the Bayou • Down on the Corner • Fortunate Son • Green River • Lodi • Proud Mary • Up Around the Bend.
00699802..$16.99

64. OZZY OSBOURNE
Bark at the Moon • Crazy Train • Flying High Again • Miracle Man • Mr. Crowley • No More Tears • Rock 'N Roll Rebel • Shot in the Dark.
00699803..$16.99

65. THE DOORS
Break on Through to the Other Side • Hello, I Love You (Won't You Tell Me Your Name?) • L.A. Woman • Light My Fire • Love Me Two Times • People Are Strange • Riders on the Storm • Roadhouse Blues.
00699806..$16.99

66. THE ROLLING STONES
Beast of Burden • Happy • It's Only Rock 'N' Roll (But I Like It) • Miss You • Shattered • She's So Cold • Start Me Up • Tumbling Dice.
00699807..$16.99

67. BLACK SABBATH
Black Sabbath • Children of the Grave • Iron Man • N.I.B. • Paranoid • Sabbath, Bloody Sabbath • Sweet Leaf • War Pigs (Interpolating Luke's Wall).
00699808..$16.99

68. PINK FLOYD – DARK SIDE OF THE MOON
Any Colour You Like • Brain Damage • Breathe • Eclipse • Money • Time • Us and Them.
00699809..$16.99

69. ACOUSTIC FAVORITES
Against the Wind • Band on the Run • Free Fallin' • Have You Ever Seen the Rain? • Love the One You're With • Maggie May • Melissa • Mrs. Robinson.
00699810..$14.95

71. CHRISTIAN ROCK
All Around Me • Be My Escape • Come on Back to Me • Hands and Feet • Million Pieces • Strong Tower • Tonight • We Are One Tonight.
00699824..$14.95

72. ACOUSTIC '90s
All Apologies • Daughter • Disarm • Heaven Beside You • My Friends • Name • What I Got • The World I Know.
00699827..$14.95

74. PAUL BALOCHE
Above All • All the Earth Will Sing Your Praises • Because of Your Love • My Reward • Offering • Open the Eyes of My Heart • Praise Adonai • Rise up and Praise Him.
00699831..$14.95

75. TOM PETTY
American Girl • I Won't Back Down • Into the Great Wide Open • Learning to Fly • Mary Jane's Last Dance • Refugee • Runnin' Down a Dream • You Don't Know How It Feels.
00699882..$16.99

76. COUNTRY HITS
Alcohol • Beer for My Horses • Honky Tonk Badonkadonk • It's Five O'Clock Somewhere • Lot of Leavin' Left to Do • Me and My Gang • Pickin' Wildflowers • Summertime.
00699884..$14.95

78. NIRVANA
All Apologies • Come As You Are • Dumb • Heart Shaped Box • In Bloom • Lithium • Rape Me • Smells like Teen Spirit.
00700132..$14.95

88. ACOUSTIC ANTHOLOGY
Don't Ask Me Why • Give a Little Bit • Jack and Diane • The Joker • Midnight Rider • Rocky Raccoon • Walk on the Wild Side • and more.
00700175..$19.95

81. ROCK ANTHOLOGY
Barracuda • Can't Get Enough • Don't Fear the Reaper • Free Ride • Hurts So Good • I Need to Know • Rhiannon • Sultans of Swing • and more.
00700176..$22.99

82. EASY ROCK SONGS
Bad Case of Loving You • Bang a Gong (Get It On) • I Can't Explain • I Love Rock 'N Roll • La Bamba • Mony, Mony • Should I Stay or Should I Go • Twist and Shout.
00700177..$12.99

83. THREE CHORD SONGS
Bye Bye Love • Gloria • I Fought the Law • Love Me Do • Mellow Yellow • Stir It Up • Willie and the Hand Jive • You Don't Mess Around with Jim.
00700178..$12.99

86. BOSTON
Don't Look Back • Long Time • More Than a Feeling • Party • Peace of Mind • Rock & Roll Band • Smokin' • We're Ready.
00700465 ....$16.99

96. THIRD DAY
Blackbird • Call My Name • Consuming Fire • My Hope Is You • Nothing Compares • Tunnel • You Are Mine • Your Love Oh Lord.
00700560..$14.95

97. ROCK BAND
Are You Gonna Be My Girl • Black Hole Sun • Creep • Dani California • In Bloom • Learn to Fly • Say It Ain't So • When You Were Young.
00700703..$14.99

98. ROCK BAND
Ballroom Blitz • Detroit Rock City • Don't Fear the Reaper • Highway Star • Mississippi Queen • Should I Stay or Should I Go • Suffragette City • Train Kept A-Rollin'.
00700704..$14.95

Prices, contents, and availability subject to change without notice.

FOR MORE INFORMATION,
SEE YOUR LOCAL MUSIC DEALER,
OR WRITE TO:

HAL•LEONARD®
CORPORATION
7777 W. BLUEMOUND RD. P.O. BOX 13819
MILWAUKEE, WISCONSIN 53213

**For complete songlists,
visit Hal Leonard online at
www.halleonard.com**

0509

RECORDED VERSIONS®
The Best Note-For-Note Transcriptions Available

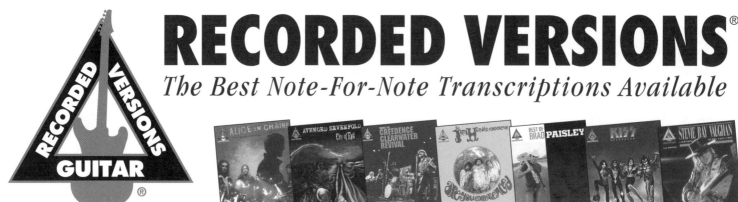

ALL BOOKS INCLUDE TABLATURE

00692015 Aerosmith – Greatest Hits $22.95	00690793 John Lee Hooker Anthology $24.99	00690631 Rolling Stones – Guitar Anthology.................$27.95
00690178 Alice in Chains – Acoustic...........................$19.95	00690692 Billy Idol – Very Best of $19.95	00694976 Rolling Stones – Some Girls $22.95
00694865 Alice in Chains – Dirt...................................$19.95	00690688 Incubus – A Crow Left of the Murder...........$19.95	00690264 The Rolling Stones – Tattoo You $19.95
00690812 All American Rejects – Move Along..............$19.95	00690544 Incubus – Morningview.................................$19.95	00690685 David Lee Roth – Eat 'Em and Smile............$19.95
00694932 Allman Brothers Band – Volume 1 ....$24.95	00690790 Iron Maiden Anthology $24.99	00690942 David Lee Roth and the
00694933 Allman Brothers Band – Volume 2 ....$24.95	00690721 Jet – Get Born..$19.95	Songs of Van Halen $19.95
00694934 Allman Brothers Band – Volume 3 ....$24.95	00690684 Jethro Tull – Aqualung.................................$19.95	00690031 Santana's Greatest Hits $19.95
00690865 Atreyu – A Deathgrip on Yesterday $19.95	00690959 John5 – Requiem $22.95	00690566 Scorpions – Best of $19.95
00690609 Audioslave $19.95	00690814 John5 – Songs for Sanity $19.95	00690604 Bob Seger – Guitar Collection.....................$19.95
00690820 Avenged Sevenfold – City of Evil $24.95	00690751 John5 – Vertigo $19.95	00690803 Kenny Wayne Shepherd Band – Best of........$19.95
00690366 Bad Company – Original Anthology $19.95	00690845 Eric Johnson – Bloom $19.95	00690968 Shinedown – The Sound of Madness $22.99
00690503 Beach Boys – Very Best of $19.95	00690846 Jack Johnson and Friends – Sing-A-Longs and	00690813 Slayer – Guitar Collection $19.95
00690489 Beatles – 1 ....$24.95	Lullabies for the Film Curious George $19.95	00690530 Slipknot – Iowa $19.95
00694832 Beatles – For Acoustic Guitar......................$22.95	00690271 Robert Johnson – New Transcriptions $24.95	00690733 Slipknot – Vol. 3 (The Subliminal Verses) $22.99
00690110 Beatles – White Album (Book 1) $19.95	00699131 Janis Joplin – Best of $22.99	00120004 Steely Dan – Best of....................................$24.95
00692385 Chuck Berry $19.95	00690427 Judas Priest – Best of $19.95	00694921 Steppenwolf – Best of $22.95
00690835 Billy Talent $19.95	00690742 The Killers – Hot Fuss $19.95	00690655 Mike Stern – Best of $19.95
00690901 Best of Black Sabbath $19.95	00694903 Kiss – Best of $24.95	00690877 Stone Sour – Come What(ever) May $19.95
00690831 blink-182 – Greatest Hits $19.95	00690355 Kiss – Destroyer $16.95	00690520 Styx Guitar Collection.................................$19.95
00690913 Boston $19.95	00690930 Korn $19.95	00120081 Sublime...$19.95
00690932 Boston – Don't Look Back $19.99	00690834 Lamb of God – Ashes of the Wake $19.95	00120122 Sublime – 40oz. to Freedom $19.95
00690491 David Bowie – Best of..................................$19.95	00690875 Lamb of God – Sacrament $19.95	00690929 Sum 41 – Underclass Hero $19.95
00690873 Breaking Benjamin – Phobia.......................$19.95	00690823 Ray LaMontagne – Trouble $19.95	00690767 Switchfoot – The Beautiful Letdown $19.95
00690451 Jeff Buckley – Collection $24.95	00690679 John Lennon – Guitar Collection $19.95	00690830 System of a Down – Hypnotize $19.95
00690957 Bullet for My Valentine – Scream Aim Fire....$19.95	00690781 Linkin Park – Hybrid Theory $22.95	00690799 System of a Down – Mezmerize $19.95
00690590 Eric Clapton – Anthology.............................$29.95	00690743 Los Lonely Boys $19.95	00690531 System of a Down – Toxicity $19.95
00690415 Clapton Chronicles – Best of Eric Clapton.....$18.95	00690720 Lostprophets – Start Something $19.95	00694824 James Taylor – Best of.................................$16.95
00690936 Eric Clapton – Complete Clapton $29.95	00694954 Lynyrd Skynyrd – New Best of $19.95	00690871 Three Days Grace – One-X $19.95
00690074 Eric Clapton – The Cream of Clapton $24.95	00690577 Yngwie Malmsteen – Anthology $24.95	00690737 3 Doors Down – The Better Life $22.95
00694869 Eric Clapton – Unplugged............................$22.95	00690754 Marilyn Manson – Lest We Forget $19.95	00690683 Robin Trower – Bridge of Sighs $19.95
00690162 The Clash – Best of $19.95	00694956 Bob Marley– Legend $19.95	00699191 U2 – Best of: 1980-1990 ....$19.95
00690828 Coheed & Cambria – Good Apollo I'm	00694945 Bob Marley– Songs of Freedom $24.95	00690732 U2 – Best of: 1990-2000 ....$19.95
Burning Star, IV, Vol. 1: From Fear	00690657 Maroon5 – Songs About Jane $19.95	00660137 Steve Vai – Passion & Warfare.....................$24.95
Through the Eyes of Madness $19.95	00120080 Don McLean – Songbook $19.95	00690116 Stevie Ray Vaughan – Guitar Collection $24.95
00690593 Coldplay – A Rush of Blood to the Head $19.95	00694951 Megadeth – Rust in Peace $22.95	00660058 Stevie Ray Vaughan –
00690962 Coldplay – Viva La Vida $19.95	00690951 Megadeth – United Abominations $22.99	Lightnin' Blues 1983-1987.........................$24.95
00690819 Creedence Clearwater Revival – Best of $22.95	00690505 John Mellencamp – Guitar Collection $19.95	00694835 Stevie Ray Vaughan – The Sky Is Crying $22.95
00690648 The Very Best of Jim Croce $19.95	00690646 Pat Metheny – One Quiet Night $19.95	00690015 Stevie Ray Vaughan – Texas Flood...............$19.95
00690613 Crosby, Stills & Nash – Best of $22.95	00690558 Pat Metheny – Trio: 99>00.........................$19.95	00690772 Velvet Revolver – Contraband $22.95
00690967 Death Cab for Cutie – Narrow Stairs $22.99	00690040 Steve Miller Band – Young Hearts.................$19.95	00690071 Weezer (The Blue Album) $19.95
00690289 Deep Purple – Best of $17.95	00694883 Nirvana – Nevermind $19.95	00690966 Weezer – (Red Album) $19.99
00690784 Def Leppard – Best of $19.95	00690026 Nirvana – Unplugged in New York $19.95	00690447 The Who – Best of $24.95
00690347 The Doors – Anthology..................................$22.95	00690807 The Offspring – Greatest Hits......................$19.95	00690916 The Best of Dwight Yoakam $19.95
00690348 The Doors – Essential Guitar Collection........$16.95	00694847 Ozzy Osbourne – Best of..............................$22.95	00690905 Neil Young – Rust Never Sleeps $19.95
00690810 Fall Out Boy – From Under the Cork Tree.....$19.95	00690399 Ozzy Osbourne – Ozzman Cometh $19.95	00690623 Frank Zappa – Over-Nite Sensation $19.95
00690664 Fleetwood Mac – Best of...............................$19.95	00690933 Best of Brad Paisley $22.95	00690589 ZZ Top Guitar Anthology..............................$24.95
00690870 Flyleaf..$19.95	00690866 Panic! At the Disco –	
00690931 Foo Fighters – Echoes, Silence,	A Fever You Can't Sweat Out $19.95	
Patience & Grace $19.95	00690938 Christopher Parkening –	
00690808 Foo Fighters – In Your Honor.......................$19.95	Duets & Concertos $24.99	Prices and availability subject to change without notice.
00690805 Robben Ford – Best of...................................$19.95	00694855 Pearl Jam – Ten...$19.95	Some products may not be available outside the U.S.A.
00694920 Free – Best of $19.95	00690439 A Perfect Circle – Mer De Noms $19.95	
00690848 Godsmack – IV..$19.95	00690499 Tom Petty – Definitive Guitar Collection........$19.95	
00690601 Good Charlotte –	00690428 Pink Floyd – Dark Side of the Moon $19.95	
The Young and the Hopeless....................$19.95	00690789 Poison – Best of $19.95	
00690943 The Goo Goo Dolls – Greatest Hits	00693864 The Police – Best of......................................$19.95	
Volume 1: The Singles $22.95	00694975 Queen – Greatest Hits $24.95	
00694854 Buddy Guy – Damn Right,	00690670 Queensryche – Very Best of $19.95	
I've Got the Blues $19.95	00690878 The Raconteurs – Broken Boy Soldiers $19.95	
00690840 Ben Harper – Both Sides of the Gun $19.95	00694910 Rage Against the Machine $19.95	
00694798 George Harrison – Anthology $19.95	00690055 Red Hot Chili Peppers –	
00690841 Scott Henderson – Blues Guitar Collection ..$19.95	Blood Sugar Sex Magik $19.95	
00692930 Jimi Hendrix – Are You Experienced?...........$24.95	00690584 Red Hot Chili Peppers – By the Way.............$19.95	
00692931 Jimi Hendrix – Axis: Bold As Love................$22.95	00690852 Red Hot Chili Peppers –	
00692932 Jimi Hendrix – Electric Ladyland $24.95	Stadium Arcadium $24.95	
00690017 Jimi Hendrix – Live at Woodstock................$24.95	00690511 Django Reinhardt – Definitive Collection $19.95	
00690602 Jimi Hendrix – Smash Hits............................$24.99	00690779 Relient K – MMHMM $19.95	

0509